"The Object Lessons series achieves something very close to magic: the books take ordinary—even banal—objects and animate them with a rich history of invention, political struggle, science, and popular mythology. Filled with fascinating details and conveyed in sharp, accessible prose, the books make the everyday world come to life. Be warned: once you've read a few of these, you'll start walking around your house, picking up random objects, and musing aloud: 'I wonder what the story is behind this thing?'"

Steven Johnson, author of *Where Good Ideas Come From* and *How We Got to Now*

"Object Lessons describes themselves as 'short, beautiful books,' and to that, I'll say, amen. . . . If you read enough Object Lessons books, you'll fill your head with plenty of trivia to amaze and annoy your friends and loved ones—caution recommended on pontificating on the objects surrounding you. More importantly, though . . . they inspire us to take a second look at parts of the everyday that we've taken for granted. These are not so much lessons about the objects themselves, but opportunities for self-reflection and storytelling. They remind us that we are surrounded by a wondrous world, as long as we care to look."

John Warner, *The Chicago Tribune*

"Besides being beautiful little hand-sized objects themselves, showcasing exceptional writing, the wonder of these books is that they exist at all . . . Uniformly excellent, engaging, thought-provoking, and informative."

Jennifer Bort Yacovissi, *Washington Independent Review of Books*

". . . edifying and entertaining . . . perfect for slipping in a pocket and pulling out when life is on hold."

Sarah Murdoch, *Toronto Star*

"For my money, Object Lessons is the most consistently interesting nonfiction book series in America."

Megan Volpert, *PopMatters*

"[W]itty, thought-provoking, and poetic . . . These little books are a page-flipper's dream."

John Timpane, *The Philadelphia Inquirer*

"Though short, at roughly 25,000 words apiece, these books are anything but slight."

Marina Benjamin, *New Statesman*

"The joy of the series, of reading *Remote Control*, *Golf Ball*, *Driver's License*, *Drone*, *Silence*, *Glass*, *Refrigerator*, *Hotel*, and *Waste* . . . in quick succession, lies in encountering the various turns through which each of their authors has been put by his or her object. . . . The object predominates, sits squarely center stage, directs the action. The object decides the genre, the chronology, and the limits of the study. Accordingly, the author has to take her cue from the *thing* she chose or that chose her. The result is a wonderfully uneven series of books, each one a *thing* unto itself."

Julian Yates, *Los Angeles Review of Books*

"The Object Lessons series has a beautifully simple premise. Each book or essay centers on a specific object. This can be mundane or unexpected, humorous or politically timely. Whatever the subject, these descriptions reveal the rich worlds hidden under the surface of things."

Christine Ro, *Book Riot*

". . . a sensibility somewhere between Roland Barthes and Wes Anderson."

Simon Reynolds, author of *Retromania: Pop Culture's Addiction to Its Own Past*

OBJECTLESSONS

A book series about the hidden lives of ordinary things.

Series Editors:

Ian Bogost and Christopher Schaberg

In association with

LOYOLA UNIVERSITY NEW ORLEANS

Washington University in St. Louis

BOOKS IN THE SERIES

Alarm by Alice Bennett
Bird by Erik Anderson
Blackface by Ayanna Thompson
Blanket by Kara Thompson
Blue Jeans by Carolyn Purnell
Bookshelf by Lydia Pyne
Bread by Scott Cutler Shershow
Bulletproof Vest by Kenneth R. Rosen
Burger by Carol J. Adams
Cell Tower by Steven E. Jones
Cigarette Lighter by Jack Pendarvis
Coffee by Dinah Lenney
Compact Disc by Robert Barry
Doctor by Andrew Bomback
Doll Maria Teresa Hart
Driver's License by Meredith Castile
Drone by Adam Rothstein
Dust by Michael Marder
Earth by Jeffrey Jerome Cohen and Linda T. Elkins-Tanton
Egg by Nicole Walker
Email by Randy Malamud
Environment by Rolf Halden
Exit by Laura Waddell
Eye Chart by William Germano
Fat by Hanne Blank
Fake by Kati Stevens
Football by Mark Yakich
Gin by Shonna Milliken Humphrey
Glass by John Garrison
Glitter by Nicole Seymour
Golf Ball by Harry Brown
Grave Allison C. Meier
Hair by Scott Lowe
Hashtag by Elizabeth Losh
High Heel by Summer Brennan
Hood by Alison Kinney
Hotel by Joanna Walsh
Hyphen by Pardis Mahdavi
Jet Lag by Christopher J. Lee
Luggage by Susan Harlan
Magazine by Jeff Jarvis
Magnet by Eva Barbarossa
Mushroom by Sara Rich
Ocean by Steve Mentz
Office by Sheila Liming
OK by Michelle McSweeney
Password by Martin Paul Eve
Perfume by Megan Volpert
Personal Stereo by Rebecca Tuhus-Dubrow
Phone Booth by Ariana Kelly
Pill by Robert Bennett
Political Sign by Tobias Carroll
Potato by Rebecca Earle
Pregnancy Test by Karen Weingarten
Questionnaire by Evan Kindley
Recipe by Lynn Z. Bloom
Refrigerator by Jonathan Rees
Remote Control by Caetlin Benson-Allott
Rust by Jean-Michel Rabaté
Scream by Michael J. Seidlinger
Sewer by Jessica Leigh Hester
Shipping Container by Craig Martin
Shopping Mall by Matthew Newton
Signature by Hunter Dukes
Silence by John Biguenet
Skateboard by Jonathan Russell Clark
Snake by Erica Wright
Sock by Kim Adrian
Souvenir by Rolf Potts
Spacecraft by Timothy Morton
Sticker by Henry Hoke
Stroller by Amanda Parrish Morgan
Traffic by Paul Josephson
Tree by Matthew Battles
Trench Coat by Jane Tynan
Tumor by Anna Leahy
TV by Susan Bordo
Veil by Rafia Zakaria
Waste by Brian Thill
Whale Song by Margret Grebowicz
Wine Meg Bernhard
Air Conditioning by Hsuan L. Hsu (Forthcoming)
Bicycle by Jonathan Maskit (Forthcoming)
Concrete Stephen Parnell (Forthcoming)
Fist by nelle mills (Forthcoming)
Fog by Stephen Sparks (Forthcoming)
Train by A. N. Devers (Forthcoming)

magazine

JEFF JARVIS

BLOOMSBURY ACADEMIC
NEW YORK • LONDON • OXFORD • NEW DELHI • SYDNEY

BLOOMSBURY ACADEMIC
Bloomsbury Publishing Inc
1385 Broadway, New York, NY 10018, USA
50 Bedford Square, London, WC1B 3DP, UK
29 Earlsfort Terrace, Dublin 2, Ireland

First published in the United States of America 2024

Cover design by Alice Marwick

Library of Congress Cataloging-in-Publication Data

Names: Jarvis, Jeff, 1954- author.
Title: Magazine / Jeff Jarvis.
Description: New York : Bloomsbury Academic, 2023. | Series: Object lessons | Includes bibliographical references and index. | Summary: "The magazine's heyday—its century–as the arbiter of culture is over, and so it is time to pay tribute to its voice, aesthetic, influence, frequent tackiness, and monumental ego as an object of envy"— Provided by publisher.
Identifiers: LCCN 2023011675 (print) | LCCN 2023011676 (ebook) | ISBN 9781501394959 (paperback) | ISBN 9781501394966 (epub) | ISBN 9781501394973 (pdf)
Subjects: LCSH: American periodicals—History. | Periodicals—History.
Classification: LCC PN4877 .J37 2023 (print) | LCC PN4877 (ebook) | DDC 051—dc23/eng/20230606
LC record available at https://lccn.loc.gov/2023011675
LC ebook record available at https://lccn.loc.gov/2023011676

ISBN: PB: 978-1-5013-9495-9
ePDF: 978-1-5013-9497-3
eBook: 978-1-5013-9496-6

Series: Object Lessons

Typeset by Deanta Global Publishing Services, Chennai, India
Printed and bound in Great Britain

For my magazine mentors:
Pat Ryan, Joan Feeney, Steve Newhouse,
Rochelle Udell, Anthea Disney, Peter Travers

CONTENTS

1 The End 1

2 The Beginning of the End 13

3 The Beginning 43

4 Magazines' Golden Century 61

5 Inside the Gilded Factory 79

6 Tangled in the Web 91

7 Next 115

Notes 133

Bibliography 139

Index 141

1 THE END

Slick. What sets magazines apart from their printed brethren is their gloss. Newsprint is coarse, dull, flimsy, and cheap: pulp. The best book stock is made to give the tactile impression of a dowager's fine linen stationery, as if ready to take type's bite on a hand-pulled letterpress. But magazine paper is smooth and shiny, industrial and modern. The stock is coated with kaolin, a white clay, to fill gaps around the wood or cotton fibers and create a perfectly even surface. Kaolin comes out of the ground—much of it mined in Sandersville, Georgia, the Kaolin Capital of the World—contaminated with traces of uranium and thorium.[1] Thus magazines are ever so slightly radioactive, which is appropriate, as the form is proving to have a half-life.

Magazines are printed on slick stock so ink will not soak and spread into the fiber of paper, as it does in newspapers, but will set on the surface, making photographs sharp and colors vibrant. Since the latter half of the nineteenth century, magazines have been as much about imagery as words. The photographs in them have been bespoke, assigned, styled, and shot by star-artistes at great expense for the exclusive use of the periodical, setting a visual tone, an identifiable aesthetic. They are meant to impress and amaze with each turn of the page, taking us where the editor and photographer wish us to go.

Of course, the words are slick, too. Some magazines—the *New Yorker, Vanity Fair*, the old *Esquire*—are the products of auteur-editors who craft their lists of contributors as a hostess would an enviable dinner party where no one gets too tipsy, where the entire table keeps silent during soliloquies, where every bon mot is quotable. Others—like the newsmagazines of Time Inc. or the *Economist* or the women's magazines of Condé Nast and Hearst in the day—were instead products of an editorial dairy farm where writers' raw milk was skimmed of its cream, heated up, and homogenized so it all tastes familiarly smooth.

The ads are slick. That's why they are there—so editorial authority rubs off on them and so the products they are selling, in turn, reveal the magazine's taste and class, high or low. Magazine advertisements broke open newspapers' typographical gridlock of dull, ceaseless text, astounding readers with big and bold fonts, illustration, and blessed white space, giving permission to periodical designers to do likewise. In magazines, national brands were born alongside the consumer economy and the mass market.

The covers are the slickest of everything, calling out for us to pick them up, to feel the thicker stock and new-car sheen that results from spreading a chemical coating of dubious recyclability atop the printed paper. Often, the coating is cured instantly under ultraviolet light in the press so the machine can continue running at high speed. Some really luxurious magazines—or actually tacky little publications that want to tart up—treat their covers with a plastic film that makes thumbing them feel like dealing a brand-new ace of diamonds. The cover image is the product of brutal competition among subjects and countless photos, having survived the trials of editorial argument and, often, consumer testing. The words—the cover billings—are worked over like a criminal under interrogation, changed and tried and tested in meetings and mirrored focus group line-ups to answer only one question: Will it sell?

Newsstands, when we still had them, were like dog pounds, where orphaned animals begged to be taken home. The newspaper's front page scolds: *You really should buy me, you know.* A book's cover beckons: *I am worthy of your interest, time, and money, don't you think?* A supermarket tabloid—the newspaper of ill repute—shouts, *BUY ME! YOU KNOW YOU WANT TO KNOW!* But a magazine's cover sings a siren's song: *Come. Listen to me. We will have a good time together. You deserve me.* Magazines seduce.

Magazines fill particular roles in media culture, roles that have evolved. In the incunabular era of English-language periodicals of the eighteenth century—in Joseph Addison and Richard Steele's *Tatler* and *Spectator* and Edward Cave's *Gentleman's Magazine* in London, then Ben Franklin's *General Magazine* and Noah Webster's *American Magazine* in America—they shaped a purported public sphere. Magazines were the feedback loop that sparked and carried conversations over coffee. Magazines *were* coffeehouses. In the mid-nineteenth century, the time of *Harper's*, the *Atlantic*, and *Scientific American* in the United States, magazines began curating the best of content from a growing abundance of media; reporting on dizzying progress in technology, industry, politics, and society; and nurturing new voices in fiction and verse, giving birth to a national literature. In the twentieth century, magazines became corporate agents of mass media, arbiters of style, gatekeepers to audience, Frankensteins of celebrity, handmaidens to brands. And in the twenty-first century? We'll get to that.

Through their many forms, magazines performed critical functions in the gestation of culture. They have always sought to gather the best writers, writing, and ideas. They tried and sometimes succeeded in setting standards, high bars of quality in language, thought, and fashion. They had the hubris to declare what was important and worthy of our attention. They prided themselves on inciting and informing—though not often hearing—the public conversation. They filled our eyes and hours with beauty. They packaged and polished and promoted. Halfway through their history and until their fall, their work was supported as much by advertisers as readers. They were highly commercial enterprises.

* * *

I loved magazines. I bought them by the pound. Hudson newsstands across New York City double-bagged my hauls a few times a week. I would leaf through them like a pirate fondling booty, absorbing the ideas and images and words and what could sometimes aspire to art. They taught me, amused me, impressed me, inspired me, irritated me, and filled my leisure in the years before "browsing" became a verb the web redefined.

Through the years, I bought cultural magazines—the *New Yorker, Harper's,* the *Atlantic*; countercultural magazines—*Ramparts, Evergreen Review, Spy, Mother Jones*; entertainment magazines—*Rolling Stone, Premiere, TV Guide*; food magazines to dine vicariously, for I am not a cook—*Gourmet, Bon Appétit, Eating Well*; fitness magazines—*Men's Health, Runner's World*, Europe's *Fit for Fun*—for I exercise vicariously as well; design magazines—especially *Architectural Digest*—though I never could afford what I coveted in it; tech magazines—*Byte, Wired, PC*, the *Industry Standard*—as I was enthralled with what would come to supersede print; travel magazines—*Condé Nast Traveler, Travel & Leisure*; fashion magazines—*Vogue, W*; men's magazines—*Esquire, GQ*; yes, those other men's magazines—*Playboy* (when I was young, I will confess, I did not buy it for the articles), *Penthouse* (I did read it for the letters), *Nerve*; city magazines—*New York, Chicago, San Francisco, Los Angeles, Time Out,* the brilliant but short-lived *7 Days*, and Berlin's *Tip* and *Zitty*; German magazines (in the hopes it would improve my slim hold on the language)—*Der Spiegel,*

Stern, Focus and a few German curiosities, such as *BEEF!*, the magazine of meat; business magazines—*BusinessWeek, Fortune, Forbes*; and media magazines—*Publisher's Weekly, Editor & Publisher.*

I worked for magazines—*People* and *TV Guide* as a TV critic and writer. And I started a magazine, *Entertainment Weekly,* which itself might have marked the beginning of the end for the preeminence of the form. We'll get to that, too, next.

So I mourn their fall and the end of the magazine's heyday—its long century—as the arbiter of national taste, style, and culture; the self-anointed conversation starter; the incubator for talent; the endless buffet of the consumption economy; and the motor of mass media. Look at magazines today. The once-glorious Time Inc. wed Warner Brothers and then consummated the worst merger in history with AOL, only to break itself up, the magazines orphaned in the company nobody wanted. It eventually abandoned the Time & Life Building, no longer able to afford rent in what one book labeled the fanciest dive. Then Time Inc. was bought by Meredith, magazine matriarch of wholesome, all-American titles including *Better Homes & Gardens* and *Family Circle*, headquartered in flyover Des Moines. Meredith in turn sloughed off *Time* to Salesforce mogul Marc Benioff, *Sports Illustrated* to a "brand management company," and one-time magazine design icon *Fortune* to a Thai business mogul. Three short years later, Meredith and the remainders of Time Inc. were bought by aging online mogul Barry Diller, the publishers' last remaining editors and writers indentured to serve on the content factory assembly line of a company called Dotdash, alongside such brands as Liquor.com and ThoughtCo. Even as its CEO declared that print was not dead, Dotdash promptly killed six print magazines: *InStyle, EatingWell, Health, Parents, People en Español*, and the magazine I had started, *Entertainment Weekly*.

Things are little better elsewhere in periodicaland. Condé Nast, the doyenne of fashion and snobbery, where I worked for a dozen years, is portrayed by the *New York Times* as a fading aristocrat, faced with the humiliating prospect of looking to Instagram and TikTok to discern the true forward edge of fashion. It is hanging on by the thread of *Vogue*'s success and the *New Yorker*'s reputation, consolidating all its international titles to lose less money. *Newsweek* has become the print equivalent of your cousin Jim who seemed like such a bright boy and was headed to college before he was ensnared by some strange cult and now is spouting loopy, dangerous conspiracy theories. *Forbes*, The Capitalist Tool, was near death when it hit upon the idea of using its gilded brand to first draw thousands of contributors who create content for nearly free, and then to allow brands to realize their corrupt dream of fooling readers into thinking their ads are content. *U.S. News* is known for little else than ranking—and, in my opinion ruining—higher education.

Look at the top-circulating magazines in the United States. Number 1 is *AARP Magazine*. Number 2: *AARP Bulletin*. Number 3: *Costco Connection*. Next: *Better Homes and Gardens, Game Informer, Good Housekeeping, People, Women's Day, National Geographic*, and finally *Time*. The magazine industry, of course, defends the physical product, its trade association churning out PowerPoints declaring that "nearly three-quarters of magazine readers love the touch and feel of print." Periodical revenue fell from $46 billion in 2004 to $21 billion in 2022. Meanwhile, Amazon reported its advertising revenue (who even knew it was in the advertising business?) at almost fifty percent higher than the magazine industry's total revenue.

And just try to find a newsstand anymore. I work in the center of the media universe, Manhattan, and it's not easy to find a magazine except in scuzzy bus and train stations, where Hudson outlets have reduced shelf space devoted to publications, treating them as a boutique afterthought next to souvenirs and soda. Stand-alone magazine stores, which used to dot the area, are all gone. The city's curbside newsstands were perversely designed to hide the covers of magazines and the front pages of newspapers and most don't even bother to sell either anymore; they are sidewalk oases offering bottles of water. In my neighborhood, only Barnes & Noble sells magazines, its racks chock full of 2,200 titles, niche upon niche—lots more, a clerk told me, in Christmas-cookie season.

This is not to say that magazines will die. Each year, a few score more are launched. Samir Husni, a professor who dubs himself Mr. Magazine, catalogs every new American magazine, which lately included *In Pickleball, Budget*

Guns, Urban Chickens, Mushroom People, Grill Girl, Hemp Grower, Cannabliss, Divorcing Well, Golf Carting, Crankshaft, Beekeeping ("All about America's sweetest hobby"), *Drew* (Barrymore), and in response to the Covid 19 pandemic, *Virus*. In a sense, the magazine form is returning to its roots: Lots of entrepreneurs throwing their special-interest efforts against the wall, though few will stick.

The magazine's golden era rose with the advent of industrialized printing technologies: the steam-powered press, stereotyped molding of pages of images and text, inexpensive paper made from wood instead of expensive linen, and the Linotype, not to mention steam-powered trains to carry magazines and their readers across the growing country. Those days are now over thanks to the next wave of technology, the internet. Who needs a magazine to sum up the week when you can read about the world from all over the world? Who wants to subscribe to magazines when you can subscribe to Netflix, Hulu, and Amazon, and be entertained for hours without the bother of reading or turning pages? Who wants the hell of trying to cancel said subscriptions? Most of all, who needs to listen to how editors distill the culture when we can hear the culture speak for itself—when we can speak for ourselves?

What becomes of the magazine now, past print, in the internet age? Legacy magazine companies and their proprietors do not fare well. They were built for a specific time and business environment. They helped establish that era and designed that economy. The old magazine editors and publishers have proven too set and stubborn in their images of themselves to adapt to new opportunities. They have become captives of their form and process and past.

The magazine is not forever. As a medium, it is a century younger than the newspaper. In the early days it was not at all clear which genre of print—book, pamphlet, newspaper, or journal—would take on the functions the magazine would eventually claim as its own. Indeed, in the late nineteenth century, when the modern magazine was born, book publishers were publishing magazines, newspapers were publishing Sunday magazines, magazines were publishing books, and magazines were publishing news.

Over their three centuries, magazines performed useful functions in society. Magazines helped readers cope with abundance of ideas and issues. Magazines fostered talent and enabled experimentation. They were conveners of community, albeit one-sided community, in which editors and writers spoke with—rather, to—people of shared interest, need, circumstance, and demographic. Magazines cemented expectations for language, art, civilization, and behavioral norms. Magazines demarcated nations and cultures. Magazines set aspirational goals. True, magazines can also be blamed for the banality of mass culture, the condescension of mass media, the epidemic of celebrity, the exploitation of base emotions, the undermining of self-confidence next to idealized beauty, and the attention economy that has corrupted the infant internet with what we used to call cover billings and now call clickbait.

Still, magazines existed because they fulfilled needs. We now have the opportunity to imagine what new forms might answer these needs. Or we might replace the form entirely. In the meantime, let us remember fondly the special place the magazine held in print culture. I come not to dance on the magazine's grave but instead to pay tribute to the institution's history, voice, aesthetic, influence, frequent tackiness, and monumental ego as an object of aspiration and envy.

2 THE BEGINNING OF THE END

I remember the day when mass media died. Pat Ryan, the editor of *People* and my mentor there, had just received the latest issue's sales report from newsstands. The omen was bad.

People was a different breed of magazine. Other hugely popular periodicals—*Reader's Digest, TV Guide*, and the rest of Time Inc.'s stable—depended primarily on subscriptions: habit delivered by mail. *People* would become the nation's most profitable magazine based largely on newsstand sales: impulse purchases, alongside candy at the checkout counter. Thus the cover was everything, ensnaring the reader to pick it up and buy. *People*'s founding editor, Dick Stolley, famously decreed seven commandments for deciding whom he would feature on his cover: "Young is better than old. Pretty is better than ugly. Rich is better than poor. Movies are better than television. Movies and television are better than music. Movies, TV, and music are better than sports. Anything is better than politics." He later appended an eighth rule: "Nothing is better than a dead celebrity." Death was thought to be too depressing to sell magazines—until *People* discovered gold in John Lennon's grave. Then deceased stars became so frequent a sight on the cover that I suggested changing our name to *Dead People Magazine*. I was joking. Another editor there was not when he proposed a new publication called *Tribute*, exclusively about dead celebrities.

From *People*'s launch in 1974 and for its first decade, picking the subjects of its covers was relative child's play. Covers featuring the stars of box-office, TV, and *Billboard* blockbusters were guaranteed winners. Until they weren't. On the day I recall, Ryan learned that a cover about *Dynasty* had bombed. Or perhaps it was *Dallas*. No matter. Hit shows were no longer working. I was *People*'s first TV critic and so Ryan associated me with—blamed me for—my medium. She spotted me down the hall, waved the sales report, and bellowed: "TV'S DEAD, JARVIS. IT'S DEAD!"

The problem, as we can now clearly see, was that new electronics—the VCR, the cable box, CD players, and the Walkman—had broken media companies' and especially broadcast networks' oligopolistic grip on the public's attention. In media's terms, the audience was fragmented. In the audience's terms, these new devices had finally brought choice and control, no longer subjugating the public to programmers' schedules in three networks or the local manyplex. Hallelujah for us! Headaches for Pat Ryan. In desperation for a new, magic formula to drive cover sales, *People* shifted its gaze from the products of the stars' careers to the events in their lives: romances, marriages, births, affairs, divorces, diseases, deaths. Bodily fluids journalism. This was also the moment when power passed from the editor, as gateway to the audience, to the publicist, as gatekeeper to the star, controlling access to interviews and photo shoots. In the unholy alliance that was then forged to compete for public attention, PR people made demands: for guarantee of the cover, for choice of the reporter, for approval of photos and quotes. The especially powerful flacks traded their stars like Pokémon cards: You can have one A-leveler if you take one of my Bs and two Cs.

It was at this moment that I sensed the need for a new magazine, one that would help busy people decide how to spend their scarce time and money on this new abundance of entertainment. I also saw an opportunity to compensate for *People*'s tabloid turn by starting a publication that would prioritize entertainment product over personality. It would be a magazine of criticism. It would not depend on the newsstand to exploit prurient curiosities but would instead be sustained by subscriptions, serving as an essential guide for audiences to get the most of the week's entertainment. On January 31, 1984, I submitted a memo:

> I'm proposing an entertainment guide, a magazine that would come to the aid of the consumer in a very confusing time. Today, there is simply too much to choose from:
>
> - Movies.

- Network TV and mini-networks of independent stations offering original programming.
- Cable TV and even satellite TV.
- Videocassettes offering current movies, old movies, old TV series, original programming, exercise, education and even first aid and dog care.
- Music on radio, on records, on cassettes and now on compact discs.
- And let's not forget books.

Yes, let's not. My sales pitch continued: "The magazine would appeal to baby boomers and yuppies, ones with lots of money and little time to spare. That, of course, should appeal to advertisers. . . . It would be enjoyable to read, newsy, authoritative, opinionated, sophisticated, sassy, talked-about and promotable. And it would be a voice for quality in an industry desperately in need of one. Finally, the magazine should be quick to start up, easy to test-market, not too expensive to operate and prone to solid growth. Just as *Money* and *People* were ideas whose time had come, so do I believe that this is the right time for an entertainment guide." I listed many possible names: *The Entertainer, The Ultimate Entertainment Guide, Choices, Time-Off, Diversions.*

Just as *Time* cofounder Henry Luce had an Experimental Department, where *Fortune* was birthed, so now did Time

Inc. employ a Magazine Development Group devoted to coming up with ideas for new titles. I submitted my proposal and it wended its way through the company's gauntlet of memos and martini-lubricated lunch meetings. Fully two and a half years later, Time Inc.'s editor-in-chief, Henry Grunwald, responded at last:

> Thanks for sending me the Jarvis memorandum about the entertainment magazine. I am afraid I am not high on this. On the surface, it makes a lot of sense, but the rationale falls apart when you really look at it.
>
> The market for entertainment is so broad that I think it is difficult, if not impossible, to create a single magazine or guide to it. For instance, the people who watch television are not necessarily the people who read books. Even if one were to stick strictly to home entertainment, i.e., the tube, there would be a lot of problems. . . .
>
> Movie reviews? Plenty of those everywhere. Besides (and this is a very minor issue) I doubt that there is a really broad market for Jarvis' vision of opinionated and provocative reviews. I suspect that the majority of movie goers don't pay attention to reviews, although critics hate to admit it.
>
> News and gossip? Plenty of that elsewhere. . . .
>
> I appreciate the enthusiasm shown by Jarvis and several others about this notion and hate to dampen it. And of course I could be wrong. But with so many other things going on, I would not encourage this project.

Those other things going on included recovering from the gargantuan flop of *TV-Cable Week*, the company's effort to publish a *TV Guide* for the cable age, with listings and grids specific to every cable system in America. It had been an exercise in Time Inc.'s favorite word: synergy. The media conglomerate owned not only magazines but also cable systems and cable channels—notably, HBO. A magazine that bridged print and cable seemed so sensible, so synergistic. *TV-Cable Week* turned out to be a complex undertaking, not so much a magazine as a database of 16,000 movie reviews and 40,000 capsule summaries of series episodes, all shuffled together by a jury-rigged computer system and dealt up uniquely for every TV channel on every cable system. Led by Dick Burgheim, the editors, who wanted to separate Time Inc. from the pedestrian *TV Guide*, built a sizable staff to produce quality features—though cable operators were unhappy if the magazine wrote about or advertised channels they did not offer.

So sure were executives of success, the company did not market-test the idea. They launched *TV-Cable Week* in April of 1983. All too soon they realized they faced disaster. Success required the cooperation of cable-system operators to add subscriptions to their customers' bills, which the companies were loath to do. Even Time Inc.'s own cable company, then named ATC, would not play along. And readers did not demand the magazine in the optimistic numbers that had been projected. After only five months, *TV-Cable Week* folded. It lost $47 million (hold my beer). Executives were humiliated when one of the magazine's editors, Chris Byron, wrote a tell-all book about the disaster, *The Fanciest Dive: What Happened When the Giant Media Empire of Time/Life Leaped Without Looking into the Age of High-Tech.* An internal post mortem recommended that in future, the company needed "a balance of experienced executives versus fast-track young tigers" so as not to be seduced by "Time's slick and formal presentations and gentlemanly approach during meetings." They decided they wouldn't indict any executive who hadn't already been fired for *TV-Cable Week*'s failure, but did vow to be tough on the next ideas.

Still, Time Inc. would not give up trying to launch new magazines. The company created a free magazine supported by advertising, *Home Office*, which came out a half-century before its time—that is to say, before the Covid-19 pandemic, Zoom, and remote work. It created the sonorously named *New York/New Jersey/Connecticut Real Estate* magazine. It tried twice to perform a limited launch of *Picture Week*, misogynistically positioned by the men atop Time Inc. as a newsmagazine for women, with more pictures than words. Harriet Fier, a brilliant editor working in magazine development, quietly decreed that Time Inc.'s male executives saw women only "neck to knees." *Picture Week* died in 1986 after losing $30 million (hold this beer, too). The development team also worked on magazines for travel, health and fitness, and nostalgia. None caught Grunwald's fancy. He wished for a higher-class legacy for his reign, so he pumped his idea of *Q: The Magazine of Quality.* It didn't market-test well and never launched. Grunwald eventually retired.

His successor as editor-in-chief, Jason McManus, wanted to make his mark by launching a big consumer magazine. Digging around, he found a few people had been suggesting an entertainment publication. It so happened that my proposal was the first. The magazine company's chief financial officer, Michael Klingensmith, had also been pushing for an entertainment guide until a vice-president told him of my proposal, which by then had gathered five years' filing-cabinet dust. We had lunch and wrote memos, which was how Time Inc. did business. Soon I was seconded from my duties as *People*'s TV critic to lead a team creating prototype covers and pages for the magazine. Such prototyping was necessary for a few reasons: First, magazine executives are a visual, tactile, and literal-minded breed; they had to see and feel what I had proposed to understand it. Second, we required sample material to use in market research—mailings and focus groups—to gauge reader demand.

Throughout the period of developing the magazine, we created fake covers about *The Wonder Years*, *Moonlighting*, James Bond, and a lamentation for the death of the LP. One featured sitcoms *Murphy Brown* and *Roseanne* with the cover billing: "KISS COSBY GOODBYE—His kinder, gentler days are past: Sweet is out, sass is in and the '90s belong to these brash and brainy women of TV." (An aside: Bill Cosby hated me. As *People*'s TV critic, I had liked his sitcom at the start but later complained with ample evidence that it had become preachy and predictable. Cosby went to the effort to find a copy of that *Murphy Brown/Roseanne* prototype, which was circulated only inside junk mail and press packets. He had a graphics shop remake the billing to read, "KISS JARVIS GOODBYE." I have his hate mail framed in my office.) We also made sample features—one detailed the backstory for every prop on *Murphy Brown*'s set—and designed pages filled with dummy copy for each review section, plus a fake table of contents. All this was used in corporate presentations—in PowerPoint prehistory when showing slides meant using a slide projector—and for focus groups. But the most important use was in junk mail.

Our prop covers were pasted onto magazines to make them look real and then plopped onto a glass coffee table with a bowl of popcorn; a remote control; stacks of hardcover books, newspapers, CDs, and videocassettes; Chinese food (with chopsticks); a drink (guessing rum and Coke); and two models' feet. The image of that table plus sample pages from the magazine were included in a large, fold-out brochure that proclaimed the arrival, from the publishers of *People*, *Sports Illustrated*, and *Time*, of "The ultimate, all-in-one guide to your very best bets in movies, video, TV, records, tapes and books." That brochure was, in turn, stuffed in an envelope with the other accoutrement of junk mail: a letter (purportedly from me), a card touting the offer (FREE VIDEOTAPE REWINDER WITH ORDER! or FOUR FREE ISSUES!), and a return envelope (SEND NO CASH!), all penned by a legendary guru of junk mail who produced breath-robbing prose such as:

> Save time. Save money. ENTERTAINMENT WEEKLY trims the fat from your entertainment diet as you sit reading! . . . We serve the best—and skewer the rest. (You have our word on it.) . . . Delectable choices and lots of 'em every week! There are certain people for whom ENTERTAINMENT WEEKLY will be a must. Are you one of them?

That went out over my signature. When people returned the card saying, "Please send me the Premier Issue of ENTERTAINMENT WEEKLY and 3 extra issues—all RISK-FREE," the company would respond saying, oh, so sorry, fooled ya; the magazine doesn't really exist and so we'll send you *People* or *Money* instead. And, by the by, would you mind terribly giving us your demographics to feed our forecasts? The practice, called dry-testing, has since been outlawed by the Federal Trade Commission as consumer fraud (you shouldn't sell what you don't have). Still, the data gave the business people justification to predict that *EW* could start with a circulation of 500,000 in 1990, rising eventually to as high as two million. That is known as a magazine's rate base, the number of copies it promises advertisers it will sell.

* * *

Now is as good a time as any to examine the business model of the soon-extinct modern consumer magazine. With few exceptions, they depended on revenue from the triad of subscribers, newsstand buyers, and advertisers. *Entertainment Weekly*, without the eye-popping celebrity scandals of *People*'s covers, was to be primarily a subscription magazine. Thus determining how much it would cost to acquire subscribers was the key to profitability. Today, as most news sites retreat behind paywalls and as cord-cutters subscribe to Netflix, Hulu, HBO Max, Discovery+, Apple TV+, Disney+ and any number of streaming services, this key dynamic of the media business, called subscriber acquisition cost, is rarely discussed.

At *Entertainment Weekly*, once the decision was made to launch, we sent out more than eight million pieces of junk mail. Across Time Inc. publications, we inserted those damned blow-in cards that fall out of magazines, hoping to irritate readers into subscribing. We invoked synergy to publish a sixteen-page sample of the magazine inside most Time Inc. titles. We bought a little TV commercial time. And we did deals—always bad deals—with subscription agents, like Publisher's Clearing House, which would sell discounted subscriptions in their mailings and keep eighty percent of the revenue. Add it all up and *EW* projected spending $24.4 million on subscription marketing to end up with 500,000 subscribers at launch. That meant we were spending about $45 to acquire *each* subscriber. That cost falls as those subscribers renew, especially after automatic credit-card billing reduced the need to send out constant reminders that your subscription is about to lapse: RENEW NOW! BEFORE IT'S TOO LATE!

Here is another factor in subscription economics that is rarely discussed: churn. That is, how many people do not renew. Depending on the magazine, as many as half do not. People who subscribe via agents like Publishers Clearing House were the worst; two thirds of them were expected to fall away, meaning we had to spend marketing money to replace them on top of spending more to grow the total number of subscribers. The basic price we charged subscribers—very common in the day—was $1 an issue. Considering that we were spending $45 per subscriber in marketing, we were already losing money on each subscription. BUT WAIT! THERE'S MORE!

EW planned on limited newsstand sales, if for no other reason than to have a presence there and expose readers to us. The good news is that we could charge almost double the subscription rate as a cover price—$1.95 each week. The bad news was that we had to share that revenue with distributors and newsstands. The worse news was that publishers always sent more copies of magazines to every newsstand than were likely to sell so as not to sell out, which meant that some goodly number of copies were always returned to be pulped. The result was that we had to print more copies than we sold—well more than a million copies, total—and printing was expensive. For most magazines, paper, ink, and printing made up roughly a third of costs. We were spending almost as much to print the magazine as to market it, more than $22 million in the first year. (This is why Time Inc.'s executives begged me to make *Entertainment Weekly* biweekly, to save on printing and postage—but I stood firm in the defense of the weekly entertainment biorhythm.) Now we were *really* losing money. CALL US CRAZY! HAVE WE GOT A DEAL FOR YOU!

And then, of course, there is the cost of the content itself. I worked up a staffing plan that called for eighty writers, editors, designers, and librarians—for a weekly, this was a smaller staff than even the monthlies inside Time Inc. That efficiency was possible because, as I said in my original proposal for this magazine of criticism, critics are like cacti: they require little care and water. For most American magazines, content made up less than ten percent of total costs. At the time, the cost of editorial content and staff for *Time* was more than $20,000 per page, for *People* and *Sports Illustrated* about $7,500. Our content at *EW* cost about $4,500 per page. WHAT A BARGAIN!

The plan, of course, was to cover all that expense and much more with advertising. Welcome to the Myth of Mass Media, which is: All readers see all ads so we charge all advertisers for all readers. It didn't matter if you skipped by the book section and the kids' section to read mostly the movie reviews, we would still charge every advertiser for your attention on the presumption that you saw every ad on every page in every section. BUT WAIT! ORDER NOW AND WE WILL SEND MILLIONS MORE READERS!

Now here's the really juicy part. No magazine charges its advertisers based on how many copies are sold. Advertisers are charged for how many *readers* there are. Therein lies the Mystical Magazine Math supporting the Myth of Mass Media. There are always more magazine readers than buyers thanks to what is known as the pass-along rate. The industry was built on the contention that every magazine was read by more than one person, and not just in the home. This is why publishers happily sent magazines to doctors' and dentists' offices, often for free, to boost their readers per copy. That is called public-place circulation. (My dear father-in-law, a Hoboken dentist, died twenty years ago. Nonetheless, we at his forwarding address still receive unsolicited and free copies of magazines that publishers think are destined for the sweaty-palmed patients in his waiting room.) If you picked up an issue at the supermarket checkout or in a newsstand and glanced through, even without buying it, you were also considered a reader.

How were all these purported readers possibly counted? Publishers hired syndicated research firms to administer incredibly easy quizzes to random consumers to come up with a formula of how many readers had seen a magazine for each copy sold. Now the numbers get to be gargantuan. *People* was the queen of pass-along. Its rate base of copies sold was as high as 3.5 million. Research said it was read by between eight and nine people per copy. So its total audience was said to number more than 25 million. That's what advertisers were charged for, on a cost-per-thousand basis. (Though *People* itself has shrunk, its rate base falling below 3.5 million, its latest owner brags that its audience is bigger than ever: its "print, digital, and social footprint" is said to be 118 million. That is to say, *People* claims a third of America as its audience because they see the brand and content on Twitter, Instagram, YouTube—everywhere.) On the low end of the reader-per-copy sweepstakes was *TV Guide*, which was presumed to stay put on the arm of George Costanza's father's couch, never to leave unless stolen by Elaine.[1] So the *Guide*'s reader-per-copy rate was about two and a half. *Entertainment Weekly*'s was pegged in the middle, at five and a half readers per copy, even though it was intended to be a resource all week. Thus, at the very start, we would charge advertisers for an audience in excess of three million. BUT THE BEST IS YET TO COME!

After disappointing the nice people who ordered our magazine, telling them that it didn't actually exist, we imposed upon their goodwill by surveying them about their demographics, media habits, and consumer profiles so we could draw a picture of the audience for our advertisers. According to the data, this was quite the desirable club. Our readers were estimated to be thirty-seven years old. *EW* would have a dual audience—that is, half male, half female. Their median household income in 1989 was projected to be $37,808 (the equivalent of $90,000 in current dollars); eighty percent were employed (vs. sixty-five percent for *People*), and sixty percent were married (what stability). The data told us our audience would be Yuppies: busy, professional, up-and-coming folk. That alone was good news, but even better, they were entertainment gourmands. Against the average American, they watched more movies, owned more VCRs, bought more new-fangled compact discs (seven times more), and even bought more hardback books (four times more). What really made my business colleagues and their ad clients salivate was that our readers watched *less* television than the average American. That is to say, they were not couch potatoes or trailer trash and they were, ipso facto, an audience harder to reach.

On the basis of these stellar psychographics we could charge advertisers $33 per thousand sets of eyeballs. My business counterpart, Klingensmith, did what publishers do and ran the numbers to project a winning proposition. Our magic formula, he said, would be to sell 1.5 million copies of each issue and 1,500 pages of ads annually—at up to $20,000 each—and we'd be profitable by the fourth year after launch. WHAT'S NOT TO LOVE? LAUNCH NOW!

Still scarred and smarting over the implosion of *TV-Cable Week* and before making a decision about *Entertainment Weekly*, Time Inc.'s executives decided they needed to do what came naturally to them: They formed a task force to rein in us young tigers and find every reason they could *not* to launch the magazine. Either the executives would play it safe and not launch the magazine or, if they did, they could say they had examined at every possible risk. The task force was headed by Don Logan, who was then the head of Southern Progress, a magazine company Time Inc. had bought. (He would go on to become CEO and chairman of Time Inc. and then chairman of AOL Time Warner's Media and Communications Group;

he will return later.) Logan brought to the task force an editor from *People*, Lanny Jones, and together they recruited more MBAs and editors. They did their job and listed every possible risk, which was not difficult, as there are always risks. They presented their funereal findings to Time Inc. executives and us. Klingensmith wrote an angry retort, telling the bosses that if they didn't want to start *Entertainment Weekly* they should hand the idea over to him and me and we'd find the investment needed.

Little did I know that there was another factor at play. Time Inc. was flirting with Hollywood and announced on March 4, 1989, its intention to merge with Warner Brothers. Then Paramount stepped in to try to spoil the marriage. While the merger battle was fought in Delaware Chancery Court, I was trotted a half-block away to show off our magazine to Warner Chairman Steve Ross and his lieutenant Bob Pittman, to get their blessing. I should have seen that we were the magazine company's dowry. I should have realized that starting a magazine that covered Hollywood in a company that was going Hollywood would be perilous. I had been warned. Pat Ryan, who had meanwhile become the editor of *Life*, told me: "Jarvis, you're not one of them. You didn't go to their schools. They don't understand your magazine. But they will use you to launch it. And then . . ." Even before the merger battle was decided, on June 30, 1989, Time Inc. announced the launch of *Entertainment Weekly*. A month later, Paramount lost in court and the merger with Warner Brothers rolled ahead, along with preparations for our launch.

I set about hiring staff. My first hire was Joan Feeney, an editor who had been employed by the task force charged with killing us. In that process, she wasn't supposed to talk with me but did anyway, asking me hard, insightful questions. I wanted her as my partner. Feeney had an unerring eye for talent and led the process of hiring editors, critics, and designers. Far more than me, she understood the essence, the soul of magazines, and kept us true to the mission we had set out. She was also an invaluable ally through all the storms that would follow. (She, too, will return in another chapter.) Klingensmith leased offices outside the Time & Life Building, a half-block from Time Inc. and a block and a half from Warner; this, we maintained, made us positively entrepreneurial. I pushed to save money by abandoning Time Inc.'s technology department to become the largest magazine yet produced on Macintoshes and the new design software, Quark. My wife, Tamara Westmark, came over from *People* to design and build the most ambitious desktop publishing network for a magazine anywhere.

Since *Entertainment Weekly*, unlike *People*, was intended for mailboxes more than newsstands, our cover needn't ooze bodily fluids. The cover could communicate that this was a magazine for real fans of entertainment, for sophisticates. Or so I believed. Unbeknownst to me, Time Inc.'s executives had been getting greedy, dreaming of *EW* as *People* the Sequel. They raised the target circulation for the first issue by twenty percent. More important, they bought expensive display positions at checkout lines in grocery stores and the since-defunct, down-market discount chains Kmart and Caldor. (You don't think magazines get that prime spot based on merit, do you? A check-out "wire," as it was called, was expensive real estate to rent.) Because my colleagues did not tell me about this newfound newsstand ambition, we were blithely producing a magazine and a first cover to signal haute culture for our au courant yuppies; the circulation director, meanwhile, was selling a flashing blue-light special competing for attention with the *National Enquirer*. Our launch cover, tied to the Grammy Awards, featured Canadian country-punk crooner k.d. lang, not a household name at the time. "At EW's launch party," *EW* writer and editor Mark Harris later recalled, "Regis Philbin looked at a blowup of the cover photo and said, loudly, 'Who's he?'"

We held that glitzy launch party for advertisers. Klingensmith had hired adman Donny Deutsch, these days an MSNBC hanger-on, to come up with a marketing strategy. "This is a great fucking idea," Deutsch often enthused. He and his team invented our slogan, emblazoned on T-shirts, cocktail napkins, and jackets: "KICK BACK. CHILL OUT. HANG LOOSE. HAVE FUN."

Our second cover featured Tim O'Brien's Vietnam novel, *The Things They Carried*. Our art department, giddy at having new-fangled scanners hooked up to their Macs, went shopping at an Army-Navy store and scanned in cloth from battlefield camo as the background on the cover.

The circulation director complained that we had the only magazine camouflaged on the newsstand.

* * *

Then began the problems. Results from the newsstands came in. With a spikey-haired, little-known, not-yet-out Canadian country crooner on the first issue and the war everyone wanted to forget on the second, you can imagine that the returns from the stores were legend. One could smell the nervous perspiration on the business floor above ours in our entrepreneurial headquarters.

Then came worse trouble. The magazine was pitched to subscribers in our junk mail promising a "risk-free"—pardon me, "RISK-FREE!"—offer of "FOUR FREE ISSUES!" Our prelaunch research had forecast how many people would order the magazine and orders did, indeed, pour in. But when it came time to pay for the year's subscription, fewer than the predicted number ponied up, far fewer. The circulation director screamed that they were canceling in droves when, in point of fact, many had taken a RISK-FREE offer of FOUR FREE ISSUES! and never intended to pay.

As it turned out, the research had been wrong about one important factor: The data predicted our audience would be older, well-employed, well-to-do, busy yuppies. In reality, the magazine's first major fans were about fifteen years younger: teenagers and college undergrads. They were youthful, unemployed, poor, and not in the habit of paying for FREE things. To this day, I hear from readers who were teens then and who loved *EW* from the first issue because it had attitude; reading it made them feel edgy and sophisticated. Cultural journalist Anne Helen Petersen wrote about what the magazine meant to her as an odd (her word) 11-year-old girl in Idaho. "As a teen, I loved the magazine's willingness to forcefully like and dislike things, a quality I rarely saw in media coverage that made its way to backwater Idaho," she wrote. "I liked that books received almost as much coverage as any other medium, and I loved parsing the differences between Video Rentals and Sales and feeling smart for doing so."[2] Years afterward, when *EW* went out of print, Louis Peitzman, a critic at BuzzFeed, would tweet in tribute: "A lot of us do what we do now because we were raised on *Entertainment Weekly*." Another responded, "Yeah . . . yeah . . . yeah . . . Got my subscription when I was 12 and have literally always wanted to be a filmmaker since then." Brian Moylan, author of *The Real Story behind the Real Housewives*, tweeted, "All I ever wanted as a kid was to work at EW." God bless the youngsters, every one. But too many of the cheap bastards didn't pay. They didn't have enough allowance. The company didn't learn of this demographic surprise until much later. When the news from newsstands and subscription payment disappointed, all eyes turned to me. I—not the circulation director, not the market research—was to blame for the apocalypse. Something had to be done.

Inquests were launched, task forces assembled. The first problem was determined to be the design. Now, I will confess that *EW*'s design was a bit too, well, sophisticated; or, one might instead call it busy and headache-inducing. As Feeney recalls, there was some *Spy* envy at work, that cacophonously designed periodical being at the time the coolest of the cool. We had too much time before the launch and I—young, without a style to call my own, and intimidated by design—had allowed the artists to keep futzing with a layout scheme. The experience made me understand how the baroque came to be: *Oh, another fillip and filigree couldn't hurt, now, could it?* I was editor; this was fully my fault.

In addition, I had broken magazine convention and opened this journal of criticism not with features but with reviews, which apparently confused readers. And we had a crooked—cockeyed—logo. The body type was decreed to be unreadable. McManus, the corporate editor-in-chief, blamed my wife's new-fangled Macs and my choice of "a goddamned post-modern font." Down in the lobby of the Time & Life Building stood a story-high sculpture of a font that happened to be the very typeface we had used, Caslon, designed in the 1730s by the first great English typefounder, William Caslon. Post-modern indeed. Nonetheless, type consultants and readability experts were called in.

McManus assigned corporate editors Gil Rogin, former editor of *Sports Illustrated*, and Stolley, founder of *People*, to harass—er, advise—me. They drew up litanies of complaints and cures, none too trivial. One of them marked up an issue circling every semicolon he could find, apparently offended at the pretense of the punctuation. In a memo shared with the other top editors of Time Inc. and the publisher, Stolley ordered: "Take date, time and network for TV Reviews out of italic, and try to make it bigger . . ." He ordered me to jettison the "bilious colors" we had chosen to label each section. In what was surely the fastest magazine redesign in history, *Entertainment Weekly* got a complete makeover by the fifteenth issue, its logo straightened up, its reviews moved back, its typeface sharp as a Dürer.

But the troubles persisted. People were subscribing to and buying the magazine by the hundreds of thousands, but not at the rate forecast in the business plan and at too high a subscriber acquisition cost. The top editors' and publisher's next target for panic was the content of the magazine, starting with its criticism. "No amount of formal redesign could change the magazine's critical tone," Petersen wrote, "a tone that Jarvis had cultivated from the start." The thirty-fourth floor—where the executives were ensconced and how they were known—quickly decided that our critics' opinions were too negative. Stolley scolded me loudly for film critic Owen Gleiberman's panning of *Pretty Woman*, arguing that the movie's box-office success proved the review wrong—as if it were a critic's job to predict and ally with the taste of the largest slice of the audience. The magazine carried on a conceit I had created at *People* to end reviews with grades, A+ to F, to guide readers through the abundance of choices we were covering. One week, Stolley went so far as to calculate our critics' grade-point average, to prove his point that we were being mean to Hollywood. He didn't wish for a bell curve so much as radical grade inflation. "A grim review of what's out there makes you wonder why so many folks are still going to the movies," he snarked of our snark. He quibbled with Gleiberman's review of Mel Gibson's *Bird on a Wire*, appealing for a C or C–, not the D the critic had given it. "This is surely a movie that lots of people are going to enjoy the hell out of."

Stolley and McManus together attacked a column critical of Arnold Schwarzenegger, one of them asking, "Are you getting an interview with him? This item could bite you on the nose." (I specifically forbade critics from interviewing stars so they would not face such conflicts.) I wrote a column in which I confessed to not liking baseball and I received a letter from a top Time Inc. business executive berating me for turning away baseball fans with my un-American prejudices. I wrote a column in which I explored Canada's new local-content law and the thirty-fourth floor went ballistic, as I was contravening the interests of our international entertainment conglomerate. It never ran and I gave up writing columns for *EW*. My colleagues from other Time Inc. magazines sensed vulnerability and pounced on me, drinks in hand, at managing-editor lunches. I had, naively, included criticism of magazines in this magazine in a magazine company, and the editor of *Sports Illustrated* wailed into me because my critic had criticized something in his publication. "Let me tell you something, Jarvis," he said, punching his finger into my chest, “I have one job and that is to protect the *brand*.” This from the editor of the magazine that made swimsuit-wearing a sport.

Everybody’s a critic. No doubt various of the bosses’ critiques were valid. The design was hyper. Critics can be pissy. But one might be excused for reading other agendas into the thirty-fourth floor’s complaints. Given that Time Inc. had just merged with an entertainment behemoth, it was no coincidence that the company’s top editors engaged in their Hollywood boosterism. I was scolded for not bringing to the top editors’ attention a piece that lamented the arrival of commercials in movie theaters, for it mentioned Warner Brothers. A music advertiser complained about a bad review, which was passed on to me. The publisher wrote to thirty-fourth-floor executives worried about entertainment advertisers hanging back “due to concern about a ‘negative review’ environment.” I tried to protect my critics from business pressure by banning ad sales people from our editorial floor.

At base, the executives’ concerns revealed the weakness of the mass-media business model of magazines. Under corporate ownership, a magazine existed to attract and retain the largest possible audience by any means necessary to sell to advertisers. A magazine of criticism—of sophisticated criticism, at that—turned out to be antithetical to the business mission of a company like Time Inc. The mostly Ivy-League editors there did not talk up to their audiences. Veiled condescension unto populism was their business motif. On the one hand, in early strategic plans, the company worried that *EW* might become too mass—too like *People* and competitive with it—and would lose its high demographics and premium ad rates. On other hand, if our magazine was too sophisticated, then it would not be big enough to hit the magic numbers of subscribers and advertisers. I confess I went into this venture not understanding what a tightrope I was walking. Eventually, I realized that I had no hope of defending my baby.

I wanted to quit. Every few days I'd ask my partner, Feeney, and a few senior editors, "Can I?" They'd say no, not yet. I stuck around as long as I could, so long as I was able to shield my staff from pressure from above. But then the top editors invited all of us to lunches in the executive dining room at the Time & Life Building, in what one editor dubbed Chez Woodshed. There, Editor-in-Chief McManus would order his usual, burned beef and gin. (He often recounted that the bartender at the 21 Club taught him it's the vermouth that gives you hangovers.) Then he, Stolley, and Rogin would berate my editors and critics for being too mean to Hollywood and too wiseacre. I couldn't protect them anymore. They were better off without me. So one Friday afternoon, as Rogin was in my office fulminating about something or other to me and Feeney and our design director, I threw down a copy of the magazine and said I didn't have to take this: I quit. No you don't, he said. Yes, I do. I hid in my wife's office until I'd been informed that Rogin had departed, after he'd wandered the hall trying to find me. Then I left the building.

Rogin went back to the thirty-fourth floor and said he'd lost Jarvis—no doubt to hearty congratulation, as that had been his assignment. I had refused to sign the Time Inc. editors' contract, as it included a gag clause and I—principled, young fool that I was—objected to the notion that journalists should sell their silence. This is why you can read what I am writing now. This is also why I did not receive the three years' salary, bonus, and benefits I would have been paid had I been fired, which they'd have gladly done. The papers reported that I quit over creative differences; quite true. The staff threw me a lovely farewell and I went to work as Sunday editor of the *New York Daily News*, which was about to enter into an ugly strike. "Man," said a wag on the city desk, "you just jumped from the frying pan to the *microwave*."

After Feeney quit in solidarity, Time Inc. appointed a smart and experienced deputy editor at *People*, Jim Seymore, as my replacement. He was one of them (Princeton) and I was glad for it, as *EW* needed someone the bosses would trust and not bully. Staff kept a pool guessing when the magazine would fold; the highest wager was issue number forty. Seymore, by one account, was under pressure to just kill the thing. But Mark Harris, one of our original hires, who went on to become a top editor at the magazine and then an acclaimed author, remembers the night not long into Seymore's tenure when he stared at an upcoming issue's pages taped to the wall and said out loud, "This magazine *has* to work." He proved to be an admirable steward who protected the beast. The thirty-fourth floor continued to pressure *EW* to become more popular, to "reflect, not lead" the culture, Harris said. True Time Inc-ers dismissed *EW*'s staff as "bohemians, potheads, snobs, and implicit homos"—and that, in Harris' view, was what made them the perfect staff. He confirmed my suspicion that the magazine's readers had indeed skewed much younger than research had foretold. "It moves me incredibly to know that we were some people's first magazine," Harris said. "We didn't realize that we were writing for the entertainment-obsessed kid in some suburban high school in Indiana. Or the one gay guy who followed everything about movies and TV in his town." And so *Entertainment Weekly* finally fell into the groove I prescribed in my original memo and Feeney held us to, helping folks who loved entertainment decide how to spend their valuable time and money.

About five years after the launch, when I was by then an online executive at Advance Publications, parent to Condé Nast, Norm Pearlstine, who had taken over from McManus as editor-in-chief of Time Inc. came into a meeting and announced, "Jarvis, your magazine is finally profitable." The room laughed seeing my shock. *EW* had gone through a remarkable $215 million before breaking even. (I'll take back those beers now.) No one would ever launch a magazine of this scale requiring this level of investment ever again. It was the beginning of the end of the era of the mass consumer magazine.

The end for *Entertainment Weekly*, the magazine, came in 2022, after the remnants of Time Inc. inside homebody Meredith—sans *Time*, *Fortune*, and *Sports Illustrated*—were sold to the online content factory Dotdash. *Entertainment Weekly* went out of print. It no longer fit in the entertainment ecosystem of the time, with choice abounding and online forums—from Rotten Tomatoes to Reddit—providing the means for everyone to be a critic.

In Anne Helen Petersen's diagnosis, synergy would prove fatal for *EW*. "Doing what its readers liked and doing what its parent company Time Warner *needed* did not always, or even often, coincide," she wrote in 2014. "*EW*'s rise, scattered identity, brilliant heyday and slow, gradual decline mirrors the same journey of Time Warner's conglomerate hopes and dreams. . . . It's not just the twilight of print. It's the end of synergistic optimism."[3]

3 THE BEGINNING

In these respects a Magazine may be compared to the sun; for as that luminary exhales the water of the ocean, and pours it on the hills and vallies, so this miscellany, draws forth the drops of human genius that lie amongst society, and as it were condensing them to showers, carries pleasure and refreshment to the plains and mountain tops, and form the rivers that flow down again to mingle with the ocean.

– UNITED STATES MAGAZINE, January 1779

In the beginning, magazines were like, well, blogs. They were a new medium—they lacked the lost plot of the newspaper, the monomaniacal focus of the book, or the pulpit of the preacher—but what made a magazine a magazine was not yet clear[1]. They were the creations of headstrong individualists and sometimes self-righteous moralists who were sure they had something new and worthy to be heard. Their mission was to both inspire and capture conversation. Though their audiences were small, measured in the hundreds or at most a few thousand, they believed they could be the wellspring of community—even of a nation. "I consider such easy vehicles for knowledge as more highly calculated than any other to preserve the liberty, stimulate the industry, and meliorate the morals of an enlightened and free people," George Washington wrote in a letter to the editor of the *American Museum*, Mathew Carey, in 1788. These early periodicals intended to curate the best of the moment's media, suddenly in abundance, scissoring up other publications and printing what they liked. They were sometimes polemical, sometimes instructional, and eagerly miscellaneous. They were doomed as businesses and died often and young.

Though a few exemplars of something close to the magazine came before in Germany and France, I mark the origins of the English-language genre with Joseph Addison and Richard Steele's *Tatler* in 1709, *Spectator* in 1711, and *Guardian* in 1713. Each was circulated, read, and discussed in London's coffeehouses, where they both chronicled and influenced conversation. Influential Frankfurt School philosopher Jürgen Habermas credits those coffeehouses as the midwives of the public sphere. Others argue that publics were born elsewhere, around books, plays, sermons, art. I might argue that a public sphere did not begin to emerge until the dawn of the internet, where the rest of society—those excluded from coffeehouses and elite and mass media—can at last be heard. "At first," Habermas himself wrote of the internet in 2022, "the new media seemed to herald at last the fulfillment of the egalitarian-universalist claim of the bourgeois public sphere to include all citizens equally." Until, in his view, it didn't.[2]

Habermas contended that the conversation in coffeehouses was reasoned and rational; it was also rough and rowdy and sometimes violent. That is why Addison, writing as Mr. Spectator, believed he needed to inform, educate, tame, and civilize public discourse. "I shall endeavor to enliven morality with wit, and to temper wit with morality," he wrote. "It is said of Socrates that he brought philosophy down from heaven to inhabit among men; and I shall be ambitious to have it said of me that I have brought philosophy out of closets and libraries, schools and colleges, to dwell in clubs and assembly, at tea tables and in coffee houses."[3] Samuel Johnson declared that "England had no masters of common life" before Addison and Steele, for they published "at a time when two parties—loud, restless, and violent, each with plausible declarations, and each perhaps without any distinct termination of its views—were agitating the nation; to minds heated with political contest they supplied cooler and more inoffensive reflections."[4] Magazine as moderator.

These first publishers didn't just speak; they listened. They trawled London's coffeehouses and clubs for news, gossip, ideas, and opinions. "In the pages of the *Spectator*, the coffeehouses are reimagined as a networked society unto itself," wrote Jared Gardner. "The coffeehouse provides Mr. Spectator with his topics, with his readers, with his correspondence; it is a self-circulating world in which a man may hope to 'Print my self out . . . before I Die,' as Addison writes in his first number."[5] Coffeehouse proprietors resented having to pay for periodicals, in part because their customers did, indeed, provide material for the publishers. And so the coffeehouses conspired to compete with the magazines, proposing a *Coffee-house Gazette,* though that turned out to be an empty threat.

Both magazines and coffeehouses concocted mechanisms to more systematically capture the mind of the patrons. In an establishment called Button's Coffee-house, Addison and Steele commissioned William Hogarth to design a lion's head into whose mouth wags and scribblers could drop their witticisms for upcoming editions. "I intend to publish, once every week, the roarings of the Lion, and hope to make him roar so loud as to be heard all over the British nation," Addison pledged. In their abortive plan for a publication, the coffeehouse owners had proposed to provide tablets with pencils attached, to be used by "gentlemen frequenters of the house with such articles of news as each may be able to afford." Thus, wrote Atoun Ellis, "the public would write their own newspapers and would be flattered by seeing their contributions in print the following day."[6] See also: blogs. Note well the threat magazines and coffeehouses—like blogs and social media—presented to authorities. Whenever more voices may be heard, censorship looms. Charles II threatened to shut down the coffeehouses, issuing proclamations in 1672 decreeing that "great and heavy Penalties are Inflicted upon all such as shall be found to be spreaders of false News, or promoters of any Malicious Slanders and Calumnies in their ordinary and common Discourses."

The most prominent heir to Addison and Steele was Edward Cave, who in 1731 founded his *Gentleman's Magazine*, a "repository of all things worth mentioning." Cave claimed to have invented the form and was the first to adopt the word "magazine"—French with Arabic roots for storehouse. He was its proprietor, Samuel Johnson one of its writers and editors. Johnson painted a picture of the editor as a choir director of sorts, bringing harmony to a wide diversity of writers and readers. Magazines, he said,

> by the materials they afford for Discourse and Speculation, contribute very much to the Emolument of Society; their Cheapness brings them into universal Use; their Variety adapts them to every one's taste; the Soldier makes a Campaign in safety, and censures the Conduct of Generals without Fear of being punished for Mutiny; the Politician, inspired by the Fumes of the Coffee-pot, unravels the knotty Intrigues of Ministers; the industrious Merchant observes the Course of Trade and Navigation; and the honest Shop-keeper nods over the Account of a Robbery and the Prices of Goods, till his Pipe is out. One may easily imagine, that the Use and Amusement resulting from these diurnal Histories, render it a Custom, not likely to be confined to one Part of the Globe, or one Period of Time.[7]

At the time, copyright as law was only a few decades old and did not yet cover magazines. (In the United States, it would not apply until after the Civil War.) Thus Cave paid liberal tribute to newspapers, books, and pamphlets by snipping items from them to publish in his pages. This was his key innovation, to make media by curating media. One could say this was the birth of the editor, in Gardner's definition: "He who could organize the growing chaos of print voices and the expanding network of information and distill from it the essence of what was truly useful and entertaining."[8] From abundance, value. In the phrase of David Brewer, publishers such as Cave created a "textual commons."[9]

Cave claimed the right to cull from others—rather like blogs, especially the Huffington Post—yet he acknowledged no hypocrisy in protesting when others copied his idea. In the quarter-century after the *Gentleman's Magazine* began, at least eighteen more London publications took the name "magazine," plus those that called themselves miscellanies, museums, and palladia.[10] Upon Cave's death in 1754, Johnson eulogized him in the pages of his publication: "The *Gentleman's Magazine*, which has already subsisted three and twenty years, and still continues equally to enjoy the favour of the world, is one of the most successful and lucrative pamphets [sic] which literary history has upon record."[11] Impressively, Cave's *Gentleman's Magazine* continued to publish until 1914.

The *Gentleman's Magazine* did garner admirers around the world, including Benjamin Franklin. In 1750, Cave published a letter from Franklin with his first reference to the lightning rod. Cave next published a pamphlet containing Franklin's papers on electricity. A decade earlier, the *Gentleman's Magazine* had inspired Franklin to plan his own magazine in Philadelphia. Franklin's would have been the first on his side of the Atlantic had he not made the mistake of revealing his plans to attorney John Webbe when offering him the role of editor. Since Franklin was putting up all the capital and taking the greater risk, he proposed taking three-quarters of the returns. Webbe disliked the deal and took the idea to Franklin's rival in Philadelphia newspapering and his predecessor as postmaster, Andrew Bradford. Webbe and Bradford then announced plans for the *American Magazine* and Franklin responded with his vow to publish the *General Magazine, and Historical Chronicle, For all the British Plantations in America,* "in Imitation of those in England." The two camps attacked each other in their newspapers with boasts, accusations, satire, and snipes until the *American Magazine* beat the *General Magazine* to press by three days.

Franklin's *General Magazine* included pieces excerpted from colonial newspapers (there were, by then, eleven) as well as books, reports on government proceedings in London and the colonies, and a few essays by the publisher himself. Webbe and Bradford's magazine lasted only three issues. Franklin's might have lasted longer than it did had he not, in the heat of competition, made business decisions that doomed the enterprise, at once increasing the number of pages in an issue and lowering the price from fifteen to nine pence, and then announcing, "We desire no Subscriptions. We shall publish the Books at our own Expence, and risque the Sale of them."[12] The risk was too great. Franklin's magazine folded after six issues.

Franklin passed the baton to Noah Webster, another reader of the *Gentleman's Magazine*, who in 1787 went to New York to found the *American Magazine*, the fifth to use that exact title. Franklin had suggested to Webster that he name it instead the *Monthly Asylum*, proposing that the form should provide refuge from the cacophony of the newspaper. Webster's innovation was to bring structure to his content, organizing it according to eighteen categories—among them morals and manners, American or European intelligence, entertainment, miscellaneous—a taxonomy of life that foretold the tidy departmentalization of a *Time* or *Economist*.[13] Webster, though a determined advocate of copyright law, borrowed freely from other publications and complained angrily when publishers took from him—not because they were stealing his content but instead his concept and his labor. Webster, said Gardner, objected to the fruits of his editing showing up in "unseemly disarray among the sordid wares and poisonous atmosphere" of the newspaper.[14]

Webster was a Federalist. He used his *American Magazine* to lobby for ratification of the new Constitution, though he opposed the Bill of Rights as he believed future generations should be free to edit their own statements of freedoms.[15] In this sense, a magazine was to him the rough draft of a constitution, a place where the leader and the literate common man—and importantly woman, for Webster wished to serve them—could learn, discuss, and discern a path forward under the guidance of the editor. Problem was, Webster found it difficult to scrounge up contributions of text and so he became exhausted filling half his pages himself. He then concocted a proposal to work with proprietors of periodicals in other cities to build a national magazine, federal itself, to help knit the infant nation together and mold its character, but the scattered publishers were wary. To this day, publishers never play well with others. Exhausted of energy and funds—his circulation reaching perhaps 500—Webster gave up after a year and a dozen issues. He had known what he was getting into: "The expectation of failure is connected with the very name of a Magazine," he wrote to his readers; "for which reason the Editor has been very moderate in his promises."[16]

Magazines were not businesses, or not good businesses. Those founded in the 1740s lasted an average of less than half a year; a century later, new efforts lasted less than two years. More than 5,000 were launched in that time; by the start of the Civil War, 1,059 were publishing.[17] Many factors made it a perilous business. Until the US Postal Act of 1794, magazines were not recognized by the Post Office and even for years afterwards—until 1845—they did not receive the subsidized rates newspapers benefitted from. Subscriptions were expensive and difficult to collect. Circulations were thus tiny, in the low single-thousands. Paper and printing were expensive. Contributors were just that, contributors—that is, unpaid and unwilling to write enough to feed the magazine's maw. Magazines depended for literary charity upon gentlemen who saw it as unseemly to write as work, or upon the ambitions of amateur scribblers. The magazine *Port Folio* stooped to beg: "Wanted. A few sensible correspondents who will condescend to clothe their ideas in plain prose."[18]

The first American magazine known to regularly pay was the *Christian Spectator*, which in 1819 decided to offer a dollar a page for submissions. Soon, Edgar Allan Poe would christen a new career title, magazinist, and fresh forms of writing also appeared. Publications came to compete intensely for prose, poetry, and eventually fiction—though at the start, in 1782, *Columbian Magazine* cautioned, "Novels not only pollute the imaginations of young women, but also give them false ideas of life." Fiction, said magazine historians John Tebbel and Mary Ellen Zuckerman, "had to struggle for general recognition in the magazine world, as it did with the public, because for so long it was lumped in with such amusements as theater, dancing, gambling, cockfighting, and horse racing. Nevertheless, fiction remained an irrepressible force."[19] Said Gardner:

> Magazine and novel "rose" together in eighteenth-century America. By the 1820s, the novel would triumph, becoming increasingly central not only to the literary marketplace but also to the national imagination and to the fundamental definition of what it meant to *be* an American. But in the previous generations, the outcome was by no means certain, and many saw reasons for

> serious concern in the novel form and the stories it told. It was within the pages of the early American magazine that alternative models would be crafted and to which a different kind of literary citizen would be drafted.[20]

* * *

According to the Pulitzered historian of the form, Frank Luther Mott, the year 1825 marked the start of a period of expansion in magazines, with a flowering of literary, cultural, women's, regional, religious, political, abolitionist, medical, and agricultural magazines and the advent of a professionalism in the field. "This is the golden age of periodicals!" declared *Illinois Monthly*.

> Nothing can be done without them. Sects and parties, benevolent societies, and ingenious individuals, all have their periodicals. Science and literature, religion and law, agriculture and the arts, resort alike to this mode of enlightening the public mind. Every man, every party, that seeks to establish a new theory, or to break down an old one, commences operations, like a board of war, by founding a *magazine*. We have annuals, monthlys, and weeklys—reviews, orthodox and heterodox—journals of education and humanity, of law, divinity, and physic—magazines for ladies and for gentlemen—publications commercial, mechanical, metaphysical, sentimental, musical, anti-fogmatical, and nonsensical.[21]

In 1838 the first eleven magazines for and by African Americans appeared, five of them devoted to abolition; almost a hundred more would follow before the Civil War.[22] A dozen years earlier, *Muzzingyegun or Literary Voyager* was published for Native Americans, mostly in Ojibwe. Trades published their own journals. Regional magazines popped up in the South and new West. Just as Webster had seen the value in serving women in his *American Magazine*, sprinkling in poetry, advice, and short fiction to appeal to them, now publishers saw value in publishing titles just for women and children. The *Lily, A Ladies' Journal, Devoted to Temperance and Literature*, was founded in Seneca Falls, New York, in 1848, a year after the women's rights convention was held there. Its founder, Amelia Bloomer, championed the fashion that took on her name but more importantly female suffrage and the "emancipation of woman from intemperance, injustice, prejudice, and bigotry." The suffrage leader Elizabeth Cady Stanton first wrote for the *Lily*.

The first highly commercial women's magazine was *Godey's Lady's Book*. Some of its pages were written by Emerson, Longfellow, Holmes, Hawthorne, Stowe, and Poe; the rest, said Mott, "was thick with sentimentality, pathos, and banality." *Godey's* continued for decades in "its rather pleasant if bourgeois way." Its editor was Sarah Josepha Hale, who penned the verse "Mary Had a Little Lamb" and lobbied President Lincoln to declare a national day of Thanksgiving. More than that, Hale supported the education of women and urged them to enter teaching and medicine as professions.

Godey's boasted of a circulation that would reach the sky—25,000—and eventually topped 150,000 before the Civil War.[23] Publishers could begin to smell scale.

Godey assured readers of "the morality and superiority of his literature" and the "purity and beauty of his engravings," offering fiction, advice, fashion for body and home, recipes, and religion. The periodical set an aesthetic ideal for American life: impossibly frilly dresses, improbably cute children and puppies with parasols, window coverings that looked like they could double as dresses, neat cottages to call home, all of which "belong to a delightful world of pure artificiality," wrote Mott. In doing so, *Godey's* also set an aesthetic for magazines, filling issues with engravings and lithographs alongside stories, with separate plates colored by "our corps of female colorers, by hand." Said Mott: "Do not call them illustrations. They did not illustrate the text; the text illustrated them."[24]

And so, the form of the magazine was beginning to gel and the trinity that would rule it was now in place: editor, author, illustrator. Editors, modeled by Cave and Webster, brought their worldviews to bear in their selections of topics, text, and writers. They offered a counterbalance to what was perceived in some quarters as the authorial tyranny of books, particularly novels. Authors, now paid and valued in a competitive marketplace and leaving the cover of anonymity behind, developed reputations and followings in the first inklings of celebrity. The curatorial mission of the magazine—to snip and share the best from anywhere—gave way to a creative instinct, to hire authors to write original material exclusive to each publication. The illustrator expanded the medium into a visual dimension, a role that would become ever more important as technological innovations in engraving and printing and eventually photography would shift the balance of power between word and image. There was, of course, a fourth at the table: the reader, whose contributions provided the audience and the funds and some of the text and authority of early periodicals. Readers would be heard from less and less as magazines took on the mantle of authority themselves and as copyright and the metaphor of intellectual property gained hold in media. The textual commons was being fenced in.

If there was a golden age of magazines, its century began in June of 1850, when leading book publisher Harper & Brothers launched *Harper's New Monthly Magazine*. Its stated editorial rationale was overtly curatorial: "The design of the Publishers, in issuing this work, is to place within reach of the great mass of the American people the unbounded treasures of the Periodical Literature of the present day. Periodicals enlist and absorb much of the literary talent, the creative genius, the scholarly accomplishment of the present age." In the view of some, particularly English authors, this was *Harper's* fancy way to say it pirated content. Before the passage of international copyright, the Harper brothers made a good business printing the best of English literature. Only later did they make a habit of paying foreign authors, including Charles

Dickens—who came to America to lobby for international copyright—for the privilege of receiving advance proofs of books. Two of his short stories appeared in the premier issue of *Harper's Monthly*.

The line between book and newspaper and magazine still was not sharp. "A good magazine is a good newspaper in a dress suit," said an ad for the *Saturday Evening Post*. "It should have all the brightness, interest, enterprise and variety of the newspaper, with the dignity, refinement and poise of the magazine." Newspapers began to publish magazine supplements. Newspapers and magazines published serialized novels in their pages. *Brother Jonathan* was founded in 1833 to publish whole novels, thus it might have seemed to be a book, but its periodical frequency made it more like a magazine, though its printing with small type on large sheets made it look like a newspaper—a format chosen to save money and to try to sneak in on newspapers' low postal rates. A few authors, too—notably Dickens—began publishing their own magazines. And now Harper's, the book publisher, was making a magazine.

Harper's Monthly soon expanded its ambition past that of a proto-*Reader's Digest* to become a formidable force in the sculpting of American culture with its own bespoke writing. It became a business success, with 7,500 copies printed of its first edition, rising to 50,000 in six months, and 200,000 by the start of the war. The magazine's dependence on its subscribers, including those in the South, meant that it chose to sidestep the issue of slavery. *Putnam's Monthly*, a competitor from another book publisher, wondered at *Harper's Monthly's*

> marvelous skill to hit the average taste of the public. This is clearly its fundamental theory. The object was, to make a salable periodical—and, manifestly, this can best be done, by just keeping pace with the popular mind. Consequently, *Harper* has no opinions, no politics, no religion, no strong expression, except of pathos or humor, because, as it wanted to sell itself to everybody, it was necessary that nobody's prejudices should be hurt.[25]

The earliest magazines had wished to provoke debate, but they sold in the mere hundreds or few thousand. *Harper's* sought sales at scale and was, before the war, allergic to controversy. "Probably no periodical in the world was ever so popular or so profitable," said *Putnam's*. Here, then, were the roots of the anodyne, accentless voice of mass media, the view from nowhere, wishing to be everyone's friend and no one's enemy, even at the expense of silence on the moral issue of the age. Before the war, ethical leadership on the issue of slavery fell to a rash of new political magazines, whose number doubled in the decade between 1850 and 1860, alongside some religious magazines and the abolitionist newspapers, including William Lloyd Garrison's the *Liberator* and Frederick Douglass' three newspapers, starting with his *North Star*.

Stylistically, in magazines of the mid-century, "heaviness was in high repute," Mott observed. But their prose improved and with it so did American writing. As decades passed, anonymity faded, authors' reputations rose, and *Literary World* praised the "compactness of structure and crispness of style" that became hallmarks of magazinists' work.[26] Alongside *Harper's*, *Putnam's*, and the *Nation*, the *Atlantic Monthly* occupied a pedestal of its own construction as the organ of the Boston Brahmin cultural elite, its most prominent writers—Ralph Waldo Emerson, Henry Wadsworth Longfellow, Harriet Beecher Stowe, John Greenleaf Whittier, Oliver Wendell Holmes Sr.—hailing from New England. As its first editor, James Russell Lowell set an example with his heavy pencil. The *Atlantic* became a patron of the American novel, *Harper's* of the American short story. Magazines, high and low, can be credited with nurturing American fiction.

More magazines sprouted up: *Scientific American* preceded *Harper's* in 1845; *Harper's Weekly* was born of its sibling in 1857; the *Nation* followed in 1865. Four high-tone pioneers—*Harper's, Atlantic, Scientific American,* the *Nation*—survive to this day, though thanks mostly to patronage and charity. None was ever a great business. Profit would come next.

4 MAGAZINES' GOLDEN CENTURY

October 1, 1893 marked the birth of mass media and its business model.

Many developments foreshadowed this moment. In the half-century after 1850, US population more than tripled and literacy soared to ninety percent. The US Postal Service expanded through rapidly improving roads and steam-powered trains and boats, making national periodicals possible. Technology enabled publishers to print magazines in unheard of volume. Steam-powered rotary presses raised the maximum circulation of a magazine from a few tens of thousands on the hand-powered letterpress to the heavens. Paper to feed these presses was now manufactured in continuous rolls instead of sheets and was made of abundant wood pulp instead of scarce rags, so prices plummeted. Then, toward the end of the century came the Linotype, the magnificent machine that produced text in complete lines, eliminating the slow, labor-intensive, and expensive process of composing type a letter at a time. The mechanization and industrialization of print was complete.

New methods of illustration transformed the look of magazines. *Harper's* was a leader in publishing rich woodcut illustrations, with multiple engravers working simultaneously on slices of drawings to speed up the painstaking process. *Frank Leslie's Illustrated Newspaper* pioneered the use of full-cover illustrations, showing readers, for example, the moment John Wilkes Booth leapt off the balcony at Ford's after having shot Abraham Lincoln. Electrotyping created duplicates of pages in metal so more copies could be printed from them. Steel engraving allowed for more detailed drawings. Photography was blossoming and then, in the 1880s came the halftone, which transformed a photo into dots to allow it to be printed alongside text rather than on separate, expensive plates, soon threatening the jobs of both illustrator and engraver. The high-tone *Century* magazine began publishing halftone photos in 1884.

The business of magazines, however, was still suffering. Frank Munsey, a humorless "bleak parched rock of a man" whose "handclasp was fishy and gave nothing," according to his biographer, had spent years trying to make a go of his weekly magazine for young people, the *Golden Argosy*, which featured stories by Horatio Alger.[1] Munsey had gone into debt publishing a general-interest weekly, *Munsey's*. In 1891, he decided that Sunday newspapers, costing a mere five cents, were dooming the weekly magazine, and so he converted *Munsey's* to a monthly at twenty-five cents. Two years in, he struggled still. "It was clear there was something radically wrong with the magazine business," he wrote. The elite magazines that existed—*Harper's*, *Atlantic*, et al.—were "made for an anemic constituency—not for young, energetic, red-blooded men and women. Editors edited those magazines for themselves, not for the people." By "the people," Munsey meant America's new middle class.[2]

Harper's, the *Century*, and the *Atlantic* cost twenty-five to thirty-five cents, selling fewer than 200,000 copies each. In 1893, S.S. McClure brought out a new monthly at fifteen cents. *Cosmopolitan* responded by dropping its price to 12.5 cents. Then Munsey planned to lower his price to ten cents. However, the American News Company, which held the monopoly on distribution of periodicals, objected, as its slice of that dime would have been too meager. Munsey tried to bypass the distributor, negotiating directly with dealers, which at last brought American News to the bargaining table. Munsey sold out the first 20,000 copies of his dime magazine, and printed 20,000 more.

Here was the beginning of a new business model for media. Munsey realized that he could lose money selling each copy of his magazine—the dime not nearly covering the cost of content, printing, and distribution—but make money on advertising. The larger the audience, the more attention the magazine had to sell to advertisers. The date of that first issue: October 1, 1893, the dawn of mass media. *Munsey's* circulation would rise eventually to 700,000. It and its many ten-cent competitors found profit "furnishing advertisers with a favorite medium for reaching the people—for the magazine reaches a class to which they specially wish to appeal," said Munsey.[3] A consumer economy was aborning with new gadgets coming off factory assembly lines—sewing machines and typewriters—and the birth of national brands—soaps and cereals and, soon, cigarettes—all of which needed to be marketed across the land. Newspapers were local and still hampered by lack of space. The *New York Tribune* even refused to take large display advertisements for fear of disadvantaging its sizable collection of small advertisers. Magazines at first included advertising as an afterthought. *Harper's Monthly* had ads, but for its first three decades the only things sold there were Harper's own books. In 1870, according to Richard Ohmann, 121 trademarks were registered with the U.S. Patent Office. Through the 1880s, only four brands—other than patent medicines—were advertised nationally: Royal Baking Powder, Pears' Soap, Ivory Soap, and Sapolio, a cleaning powder. But in 1906, more than 10,000 trademarks were registered.[4]

In mass magazines, advertisers could not only reach large, national audiences, they could do so with splash: twenty-four-point headlines instead of six-point type, now accompanied by illustrations, all set apart with the shocking design innovation: white space. With that, the look of media changed forever. No longer gray lagoons of text, print now carried impact. This wasn't necessarily the ruin of the culture one might expect—not yet—for the middle-class magazines did not patronize and condescend to their audiences. Theirs was an aspirational medium meant to raise readers up. It was meant to educate them.

It also meant to protect them—even from magazines' own advertisers. In 1901, *Good Housekeeping* founded an institute to test products. A year later the publisher announced that it would accept ads only for products approved by the institute, and in 1909 it began issuing its Good Housekeeping Seal of Approval. The old mainstay of newspaper and magazine advertising, patent medicine and snake oil, eventually disappeared.

S.S. McClure—who, like Munsey, wanted to be called "Chief"—had been scraping by trying to invent another business model: syndication, selling stories to newspapers across the country. Then he realized he could turn all this content into his own magazine. *McClure's* came to life in May 1893, at fifteen cents, then ten. The first issues were a struggle. A loan from Arthur Conan Doyle kept the venture afloat. In the end, it was the quality and inventiveness of *McClure's* writing and reporting that saved it. McClure read a submission by Ida Tarbell on the paving of Paris streets and declared, "This girl can write." He commissioned her to compose many-part biographies of Napoleon in 1894 (circulation doubled from 40,000 to 80,000), then Lincoln in 1895 (circulation shot up again to 250,000). Then he convinced this daughter of the Pennsylvania oil fields to write the story of the "Mother of Trust," Standard Oil, and its baron, John D. Rockefeller. At the same time, McClure supported Lincoln Steffens' investigation of corruption in multiple cities and Ray Stannard Baker's coverage of the rise of the labor movement, beginning in the coal strike of 1902.

"The fundamental weakness of modern journalism," McClure wrote, "was that the highly specialized activities of modern civilization were very generally reported by men uninformed in the subjects which they wrote." That is why McClure decided to "pay my writers for their study rather than for the amount of copy they turned out." Or as Rudyard Kipling said to him: "McClure, your business is dealing in brain futures." *McClure's* attracted the first reports of Marconi's discovery of wireless telegraphy and the Wright Brothers' flying machine. *McClure's* supported Tarbell through five years of research and writing on Standard Oil, producing fifteen articles, which each cost the magazine $4,000 (more than $125,000 in current dollars). "I had to invent a new method in magazine journalism," McClure declared in his autobiography. That method was called, at first disparagingly, muckraking. McClure insisted that the invention was accidental, that he had not set out to attack incumbent institutions. Yet Tarbell's investigation did result in the break-up of the Standard Oil trust and *McClure's* set the progressive agenda of the era.[5]

America's dime magazines were the envy of Great Britain. In 1910, writing in the *Fortnightly Review*, Scottish critic William Archer praised American cheap magazines as "a group of some half-dozen periodicals of extraordinarily vital and stimulating quality, which must be reckoned, I think, among the most valuable literary assets of the American people. There is nothing quite like them in the literature of the world—no periodicals which combine such width of popular appeal with such seriousness of aim and thoroughness of workmanship." Archer granted American magazines credit for the development of the short story as a genre, but said Britain had plenty of its own talent. What impressed him more was the breadth of the Americans' subject matter, the depth of their reporting, their authority earned through straightforward presentation of fact. He singled out McClure for "his feverish fertility of ideas, his irrepressible energy, his sanguine imagination. But besides being an editor of genius, he is a staunch and sincere idealist. When he determined to make his magazine a power in the land, he also determined that it should be a power for good; and he has nobly fulfilled that resolve."[6]

In America, the dime magazine had its critics, including H.L. Mencken, who in 1919 dismissed *Munsey's* as "little more than a Sunday 'magazine section' on smooth paper" and McClure as "a shrewd literary bagman" who managed to "apply the sensational methods of the cheap newspaper to a new and cheap magazine." Mencken would declare the muckraking magazine soon past its prime. Why? "Have all the possible candidates for the rake been raked? . . . The muck-raking magazine came to grief, not because the public tired of muck-raking, but because the muck-raking that it began with succeeded."[7] The powerful were brought to heel and rectitude is banal.

With magazines came a cementing of class culture in America. "Elites carried forth the 'sacralization' of art and culture: purging it of amateurism, widening the separation between creators and audiences, framing art as difficult and pure, divesting it of more accessible, popular elements," wrote Richard Ohmann in *Selling Culture: Magazines, Markets and Class at the Turn of the Century*. "Culture became a system that clearly signaled and manifested social class: refined and sacralized at the top of the hierarchy, pleasure-seeking and openly commercial at the bottom." The *Atlantic*, *Century*, and *Harper's* occupied the top. *Godey's*, *McClure's*, *Munsey's*, et al. did not occupy the bottom but instead the new, aspirational middle. "This culture," said Ohmann, "valued information, enlightenment, and elevation of the spirit."[8]

* * *

The magazine was now secure as an institution, its form and function established. Its business model, relying on reader and advertiser together, bred success. And so, the magazine grew to serve every interest—in Mott's words, "all the ideologies and movements, all the arts, all the schools of philosophy and education, all the sciences, all the trades and industries, all the professions and callings, all organizations of importance, all hobbies and recreations."[9] Magazines filled newsstands with an incredible array of publications for business, agriculture, industry, literature, women, men, children, family, pets, home, fashion, science, health, education, hobby, sport, music, radio, cinema, celebrity, humor, political persuasion, and religion. And new forms were born: the Black magazine, the porn magazine, and the newsmagazine.

Because magazines presume an ongoing relationship with readers—who could be considered a community—they also became a medium for the organization of movements. Magazines were founded expressly to organize against slavery and for women's suffrage, to promote socialism, to oppose immigration, and to inspire radicalism. In 1910 W.E.B. Du Bois founded and edited *The Crisis* out of the NAACP. It was an early and important magazine for Black America that has lasted more than a century. In 1942, John H. Johnson was assigned by his boss at the Supreme Liberty Life Insurance Company to read Black newspapers and "prepare a digest of what was happening in the Black world." Johnson was inspired to turn this into a commercial counterpart to *The Crisis*, publishing *Negro Digest* in 1942. He borrowed $500, using his mother's furniture as collateral. He convinced a magazine distributor in Chicago to carry the *Negro Digest* by getting friends to go to newsstands demanding it and then having them buy out copies so he could resell them. "Circulation begat circulation," he said. "Money, which is perhaps the greatest of all civil rights bills, was working now."[10]

With the advent of quality color printing, magazines became ever more profoundly pictorial. Du Bois realized that. "It was the rule of most white papers," he said, "never to publish a picture of a colored person except as a criminal and the colored papers published mostly pictures of celebrities who sometimes paid for the honor. In general, the Negro race was just a little afraid to see itself in plain ink."[11]

Johnson realized the need as well. “Black people want to see themselves in photographs,” he said. “We were dressing up for society balls, and we wanted to see that. We were going places we had never been before and doing things we'd never done before, and we wanted to see that.”[12]

After *Negro Digest*, Johnson published the first issue of *Ebony* on November 1, 1945. He wanted it to carry good news about Black “success and achievement in any field,” celebrating celebrity, wealth, and beauty. It was an immediate hit, with circulation rising to 623,000 in 1960, more than a million in 1968. *Ebony* benefitted from a key measurement of health in the magazine business: its pass-along rate. Read in barber shops, beauty salons, doctors' offices, and churches, *Ebony* claimed a circulation of 1.3 million in 1975 and a total readership of 7 million. Persuading white marketing executives to buy space in *Ebony* to reach Black readers was much harder. In 1947, Johnson convinced Zenith Radio to buy ads, which led to Pepsi, Lucky Strike, Colgate, Carnation, and other mass brands following. It took ten years to convince the first automotive advertiser and fifteen years to sign Campbell Soup. It took longer still for Johnson to convince marketers to employ Black models in their ads.

Korey Bowers Brown studied *Ebony* and its impact in Black culture and politics of the 1960s and concluded that “*Ebony*, more so than any other black media outlet, made it possible for large segments of the black population to become more aware and accepting of the growing militancy and ‘Black is Beautiful’ aesthetics of the era.” Through its coverage of news, its interviews with well-known subjects, and importantly its many pages of letters to the editor in each issue, "no other single cultural instrument captured the attention and displayed the multiple perspectives of black Americans during the Black Power movement in a more dynamic fashion than did *Ebony*." In this same era, *Ebony*'s pictorial predecessors, *Life* and *Look*, had passed their peaks, with more than 7 million circulation for each, and they were starting to decline as both readers and advertisers were drawn away to television. But Black people weren't on TV. *Look* and *Life* went out of print in 1970 and 1971 respectively while *Ebony*'s circulation continued to grow.[13]

* * *

Any object of censorship seeks to evade control when a new medium for expression or a new business model arises. Because magazines were carried in the mail, the federal government claimed jurisdiction over their contents. Thus magazines—especially those containing porn—became a battlefield on which censorship was fought. *Ulysses* was first deemed obscene and banned by a local court in the United States because of one chapter, which included reference to masturbation, published in the *Little Review*. Anthony Comstock, a self-appointed moral guardian (as most are) for the Post Office, called the mail (the original internet) "the great thoroughfare of communication leading up into all our homes, schools and colleges. It is the most powerful agent, to assist this nefarious business, because it goes everywhere and is secret."[14]

Comstock had Victoria Woodhull arrested for publishing details of Henry Ward Beecher's affair with a parishioner in her magazine, *Woodhull & Claflin's Weekly*. Mencken's *The American Mercury* was found obscene, in violation of the censorial Comstock Law, leading the great American author to declare the Post Office "one of the most sinister agents of oppression in the United States." Mencken said Comstock "did more than any other man to ruin Puritanism in the United States" and further contended that he "liberated American letters from the blight of Puritanism."[15] Said Mencken:

> In 1873, when the late Anthony Comstock began his great Christian work, the American flapper, or, as she was then called, the young lady, read Godey's Ladies' Book. To-day she reads—but if you want to find out what she reads simply take a look at the cheap fiction magazines which rise mountain-high from every news-stand. It is an amusing and at the same time highly instructive commentary upon the effectiveness of moral legislation. The net result of fifty years of Comstockery is complete and ignominious failure. All its gaudy raids and alarms have simply gone for naught.[16]

Comstock's ghost returns to stir up moral panic about speech in each new medium, from magazines to comic books, film to television, records to video games to the internet.

Playboy was an inevitability. Frank Munsey had printed some putatively tasteful nudes in his magazine. Real porn had to await progressing mores in society, the death of Comstock and his law, and most important, improvements in high-quality color printing on slick paper to make flesh so lush, so realistic as to inspire fantasy in pinups and then, unclothed, in *Playboy*. Sadly, I never did find a stack of *Playboys* in my father's drawers, so I needed to rely on my adolescent-of-the-sixties counterculture credentials to safely pick up and—with fluttering heart, buy—a copy of the *Evergreen Review*, which featured a pictorial of two naked women cavorting inexplicably in an auto junkyard. It was, of course, entitled "Auto Erotica." This was my first crossing of the pubic-hair line. What made magazines—men's magazines—perfect for porn was, naturally, privacy. One needn't venture into a scuzzy Times Square theater, risking reputation to see strippers or film. One could subscribe to *Playboy*, receive it safely through the mail, and read it for the articles—until the internet one-upped print.

One other invention of the period was the news-magazine (it eventually lost its hyphen), the creation of Henry Luce and Briton Hadden, two Yale pals who in 1923, at age 24, launched *Time* with the help of more white, male Ivy Leaguers. Curating another's content was, of course, ingrained in the DNA of magazines from birth. But *Time* didn't quote; it rewrote. Organizing content according to a strict structure of departments and sections had been American magazine pioneer Noah Webster's innovation. *Time* turned its taxonomy into an organizing principle for society, spawning the misapprehension that life could be as well-organized and logically constructed as an issue of the magazine. *Time* had the audacity to promise all the world's vital news in premasticated prose, fresh each week.

Luce and Hadden's prospectus was as brash as it was conservative. Sounding every bit the recently shaving Stanford graduates in Silicon Valley circa 2000, they made pronouncements about the state of the world and their power to treat its ills: "People are uninformed BECAUSE NO PUBLICATION HAS ADAPTED ITSELF TO THE TIME WHICH BUSY MEN ARE ABLE TO SPEND ON SIMPLY KEEPING INFORMED. . . . *Time* is interested—not in how much it includes between its covers—but in HOW MUCH IT GETS OFF ITS PAGES INTO THE MINDS OF ITS READERS." The founders contended their publication would present no bias, but recognizing the impossibility of neutrality, would acknowledge certain prejudices, including: "A distrust of the present tendency toward increasing interference by government. . . . A prejudice against the rising cost of government. . . . A respect for the old, particularly in ideas."[17]

As the creator of a magazine in the company they founded, I will confess to certain schadenfreude at the knowledge that Luce and Hadden's launch was rather a disaster. The first issue sold 9,000 copies, a third of their cautious projection. Half of 5,000 newsstand copies were returned unsold. Luce worried there was "no limit to the extent of the immediate catastrophe!—Not when people are already writing in at the rate of over *100* per day, telling us to cancel their trial subscriptions."[18] A leading ad agency told them their first issue should be their last. It lost money until 1927.

Of course, *Time* succeeded. It spawned copycats: *Newsweek* and *U.S. News* in America, *Der Spiegel* in Germany, *Macleans* in Canada, by some counts fifty offspring around the world. *Time* affected the language with its affect. The founders had taken Greek at Hotchkiss and Yale and, said biographer Alan Brinkley, they made the *Iliad* their adjectival model: "wine-dark sea" and "fleet-footed Achilles" begat "many-towered" Danzig and "mocking, mordant, misanthropic" George Bernard Shaw. They bragged of entering words into the American glossary: kudos, tycoon, pundit. The magazine was widely mocked for its Yoda-esque inverted syntax. "Backward ran sentences until reeled the mind," giggled the *New Yorker* in 1936.

Until nearly the end of the century, *Time*'s writers wrote without bylines—"as nuns sacrifice their hair, so Luce's writers are shorn of their names," said social critic Dwight Macdonald. He accused them of finding indirect means to inject their opinion into stories, putting their views "into the mouths of dummies labeled 'well-informed critics' or 'unbiased observers.'" In this magazine, Marshall McLuhan sensed a paradox of elitism and condescension. "*Time* readers were somehow taught to think of themselves as 'different,'" he wrote. "They are an exclusive little coterie of millions and millions of superior people." In its "tone of private gossip and malice," McLuhan found "not the formula for a world society but for clique control and indoctrination. . . . *Time* is also a nursery book in which the reader is slapped and tickled alternately. It is full of predigested pap, spooned out with confidential nudges." The Ivy Leaguers in *Time*'s offices paint the world with their "seal of haughty schoolboy sophistication." Macdonald had profound concerns about the magazine's influence. "An organization which puts ideas into 30,000,000 heads is a powerful little gadget to be under the control of a single individual," he warned. Multiply that number by 100 and we hear the exact same complaint about Mark Zuckerberg and Facebook.

Soon after Hadden's untimely death at age 29, Luce in 1930 founded *Fortune*, which was to be entitled *Power*, a magazine lush in photography and prose meant to celebrate capitalism and wealth even in the midst of the Great Depression. McLuhan was still concerned. "*Fortune* is conducted as a major religious liturgy celebrating the feats of technological man," he said. "Paeans of praise to machine production interspersed with numerous scenes of luxurious and exclusive playgrounds for the *gauleiters* of big business."[19]

The company produced *The March of Time*, a radio show, starting in 1931, then a cinema newsreel in 1935. Next, in 1936, came *Life*, which in Luce's cabernet-colored prose would meet the public's desire "to see life; to see the world; to eyewitness great events . . . to see and to take pleasure in seeing; to see and be amazed; to see and be instructed." Success almost killed *Life* as Luce at launch signed long-term advertising contracts assuming a circulation of 300,000, while he ended up paying for paper, ink, printing, and distribution for 1 million copies a week. He could have sold 3 million copies more but couldn't afford to. *Life* became

America's television on paper until TV came along a decade into its tenure. In 1954, Luce started *Sports Illustrated*, which according to company legend he stood by even as it lost money for more than a decade.

In all of this, Luce did not so much invent new magazines as he invented the media conglomerate. Time Inc. bought forests and paper mills, launched satellite TV channels and cable TV systems, published books, and pioneered new means of marketing its magazines to the masses by giving away premiums—clock radios with *Time*, the sneaker-phone for *Sports Illustrated*—to entice readers into its web. The machinery of print—powered presses and Linotypes—mechanized the process of printing. Luce industrialized the process of reporting, writing, editing, and producing words for the masses to sell them to marketers.

5 INSIDE THE GILDED FACTORY

In 1981, I arrived at the Time & Life Building in New York for a week's tryout for jobs as a writer at *People* or across town as an editor at *New York Magazine*. A *People* editor unceremoniously informed me that I was fortunate to have snuck in, for as far as they were concerned a newspaper person could not be made into a magazine person. We people of pulp were too crass and common. But fine, my host said, have a seat in that vacationing assistant managing editor's corner office (with an awesome view of New Jersey). He handed me thirty pages of notes from a correspondent and envelopes full of news clippings and assigned me to turn it all into 120 lines of text.

I had been a reporter, columnist, and editor at the *Chicago Tribune*, *Chicago Today* (a paper that had no tomorrow), and the *San Francisco Examiner*. As a rewriteman (apologies for the sexism of the title and age), I learned to produce stories on deadline. I would write a paragraph at a time, ripping each out of the typewriter and slapping it into the hands of a copy boy (to ameliorate that sexism, they were eventually known as copy kids even if they were not kids; pardon the ageism). Thereby the text could course its way through the process of manufacturing a newspaper—editing, copy editing, typesetting, proofreading, page composition—even while I was still writing. Thus I learned to write fast. At *People*, I finished the story I was assigned that morning and handed it in to a shocked senior editor. I asked for my next assignment. There was no more work to be had that day. So after lunch, I edited a *New York* story and enjoyed the view. This exact sequence was repeated each day for the week: one story each morning, watching the Hudson flow by each afternoon. At the end of the week, I was turned down by *New York* but offered a job as a *People* senior writer. As I headed out to fly home, a wizened old Time-Incer who had been exiled from *Time* to *People* for sins unknown, pulled me into his office and scolded me: "Never do that again." I had no idea what trespass I had committed until I returned and heard the boss, Pat Ryan, plead to her staff of writers, "People, we have to be more productive. Can you please at least try to write one story a week?"

Once I arrived for work, I learned much, some of it useful. I remember writing a story about an athlete's struggle with weight, making her victories and losses in dieting a leitmotif through the mere 150-line-long narrative. I was instructed that I had wasted space. I should deal with "all the fat stuff" in one paragraph to save lines for cramming in more quotes and facts. I learned the value of the dash—and overuse it to this day—for the sake of such compaction. Captions in newspapers usually repeat information from the accompanying story but in magazines, captions provide the opportunity to shoehorn in additional information. And I learned that photos are everything. I was shocked seeing good stories by talented writers killed just because the pictures weren't captivating enough. Apart from some texty, serious magazines that tend to pile up like guilt—the *New Yorker,* the *Atlantic, Harper's,* the *Economist* (which they call a newspaper but it's not)—every magazine, especially one lighter than air like *People*, is defined by its photos.

Magazines also defined themselves by their processes. Time Inc. practiced what Joseph Epstein called group journalism, an invention of Luce and Hadden. It takes a village to make a story. Here is how any article would progress: A correspondent sends in a pitch for a story or an editor has an idea for one. An assignment to interview a celebrity or pursue a trend is made by the senior editor overseeing a section, through the chief of correspondents, to a bureau chief, and finally to a reporter in the field. The reporter sends back by telex (only later fax and much later email) thirty or forty pages of notes brimming with quotes and atmosphere: fifty times what would end up in type in the magazine. A writer in New York is assigned to take that material—plus clippings from the library, supplied by a researcher—and boil it down to its *jus*. The senior editor who assigned the story now edits the bejesus out of it, often rewriting it. Then a "top editor"—an assistant managing editor by title—reads it and just as often rewrites it again. Then the boss, the managing editor (there was only one editor-in-chief over all of Time Inc. so all the magazine editors were MEs), would read it and sometimes send it back for another rewrite. Repeat steps 4 and 5, sometimes more than once. If the story is at all sensitive, it is sent to legal and upstairs to the thirty-fourth floor, where the editor-in-chief and lieutenants will ask obtuse questions and perhaps require another rewrite. They all practice canine editing: lifting their legs to mark that they were there. "Group journalism," said Epstein, "achieves nothing so much as to put the journalistic coverage of an event at several removes from the direct experience of it."[1] The point was to homogenize and pasteurize every story until it came out in the same institutional voice, the formula assuring just the right, light spice, a full quotient of facts and fragmentary quotes, as many puns as could be tolerated in polite society, and some distance, speaking always from a perch above. (Writing this, I finally and more fully recognize what a misfit *Entertainment Weekly* was inside Time Inc. for it spoke as the sum of its individual voices, not a singular voice itself.)

By now the story is a goddamned mess. Enter the savior, the researcher—most were still women in the 1980s—to try to fix it, fact-checking every assertion, marking dots over every single verified word at every step in the process. I remember a friend spending forever on the phone trying to fact check the age of actress Betty Buckley's dog. Writers and editors would often think the story needed this fact or that and, not having it at hand, would insert as a placeholder "TK" for "to come." Feeney recalls having to ascertain Dustin Hoffman's TK shoe size. Or they would insert a best presumption of a fact and add a "CK" for "check" as a means of ass-covering. The researcher is expected to get on the phone with reporters and sources and dig into files to fill in these blanks. We were all told the legend of the *Time* editor who wrote "TK trees in Russia" and the researcher dutifully came up with a credible number. Richard Stolley once had a fit over a reference to "thousands" of lights on the Rockefeller Center Christmas tree and insisted someone fill in the exact number. It says much about the structure of a newsmagazine that the providers and guardians of facts were the lowest-ranked and lowest-paid. In 1982, a *People* story about the wrap party for the last episode of *Barney Miller* made mention of Abe Vigoda—Fish—being absent (because he was out of town starring in a play). A top editor inserted the words "the late" in front of Vigoda's name. The researcher dutifully took it out. On the way to the press, the top editor put it back, for top editors do not like to be doubted. After the issue came out, Vigoda took out a full-page ad in *Variety* with a picture of himself sitting upright in a coffin, reading *People*.

In parallel with the assembly line for text, photo editors assign shoots of subjects—every star at some point pictured in the kitchen, making pasta, always pasta, to provide their just-like-you-and-me, real-person bona fides. These editors order up more images from photo agencies, bringing in piles of paparazzi pictures. The photo editor selects the best and meetings are held with scores of photos scattered across a large, standing-height layout light table so the writer, senior editor, photo editor, designer, and ultimately the managing editor can pick the winners. Designers then lay out pages with dummy type—*lorem ipsum*, et cetera—which the managing editor would tear apart as if they were scrapbooks. Designs could be sent back to be redone as often as stories. Once the layout is finalized, editors and writers set about writing headlines and captions to fit the holes, sending them back through the same gauntlet the text had suffered.

Every line written and every edit made—by senior editor, top editor, and copy editor, too—is typed and retyped into the company's typesetting system by the production department. Years later, after editors and writers began working on computers and after those computers were connected to the internet, I was called in at Condé Nast to teach *Vanity Fair* columnist Jim Wolcott how to blog, in hopes that he would. I opened a WordPress page, had him type a headline and then type a sentence below, and then I told him to click on the "post" button. I clicked another button and showed him the result, instantly on the web for the world to see. He was astounded. No editors? No fact-checkers? No waiting? Just like that? Not that he didn't appreciate the help; Feeney remembers his gratitude when she fact-checked an error in his copy. Still, he was gobsmacked at the prospect of eliminating the entire editorial process I have just described.

What was all the more exhausting about that process was that a great number of stories survived every step yet never ended up in print. On an issue's mockup, which listed which stories and which ads would appear on which pages, two and sometimes three stories competed for each slot. The belief was that this competition would produce the best stories and the best magazine. But the wasted labor was monumental and the disappointed writers, photographers, and subjects were legion. In Condé Nast's tonier magazines, editors would spend fortunes assigning stories that never ran. Harry Evans, *Condé Nast Traveler*'s legendary founding editor, was said to have a bank of assigned but unprinted stories worth $1 million by the time he left to head Random House.

* * *

A magazine is more than its end product and its process. It is also its culture. *People* was an oddity in the building, a commoner among the elite. Even so, it was staffed with multiple Ivy Leaguers—two of its editors were named Jones but neither was a Bob; one was a Cranston (Harvard) and the other a Landon (Princeton). Some were embarrassed working at *People* instead of on the Big Book, *Time*, but the fringe benefits salved the humiliation. The salaries for writers and editors were good. Expense accounts were a fungible asset, with writers and editors going out for two-plus-drink lunches every day or allegedly hoarding fake receipts to buy couches at Bloomingdale's. Three or four days a week, the work was easy. Closing nights, when the magazine was put to bed but the staff was not, were long. Lore had it that one night in the early days of *People*, Stolley turned to a senior editor at the next urinal and said, "Why don't you go home early tonight, Jim?" It was 3 a.m. Yet the long hours weren't so bad, for dinner was catered. Anyone working past a certain time got a ride home in a chauffeur-driven black car—even if home was to the weekend house way out in the Hamptons. There were snacks: a closet filled with chips and Pepperidge Farm cookies. And booze—oh, there was booze. At *Time*, stewards rolled drink trolleys through the halls. At *People*, underlings had to make do with Heineken and decent jug wine at the dinner buffet. But the *Mad Men* credenzas in the offices of senior and top editors were all stocked with hard liquor upon requisition. Top editors were served drinks with lunch by stewards in the company dining rooms and at dinner time, they retreated to the steakhouse downstairs for more libation. One never wanted one's story to be top-edited in the p.m.

The perks and the hangovers were similar at other magazine publishers uptown and down, but the politics inside each empire were unique. I spent a dozen years at Advance Publications, the parent company of Condé Nast—publisher of *Vogue, Glamour,* the *New Yorker, Architectural Digest, Gourmet, Bon Appétit,* et al. Though I had been schooled in political warfare at Time Inc. that was little help against the sterling silver shivs of Condé. There I wore protective coloration—suits that I will now confess came from Barney's Warehouse Sale—but suffered not a fraction of the pressure I observed women enduring as they were silently judged on elevators, as if on the runway. Eating in the Frank-Gehry-designed cafeteria in Four Times Square—where the patrons were supplied with pashminas should a chill overcome them and garlic was outlawed because it was said to give Si Newhouse allergic agita—was pure theater, observing the passing fashion and the self-starvation portions and checking to see who was sitting with Si that day. Hearst—home of *Cosmopolitan*, *Esquire*, and *Town & Country*—was, politically speaking, Condé lite, like getting a cushy desk job on the Western Front instead of fighting in the artillery on the Eastern. McGraw-Hill published *Business Week* but also shelves full of gritty business-to-business magazines for the oil, electrical, and other industries. They were dull business technocrats. At *Rolling Stone*, Jann Wenner placed his office on the second floor, over Sixth Avenue, so all could see him at work. Other nearby publishers—Gruner + Jahr, Hachette-Filipacchi—were mere immigrants in the land.

After leaving *Entertainment Weekly* and surviving time at the *New York Daily News* as Sunday editor before it went bankrupt, I went to *TV Guide* to renew my critical license as its Couch Critic. Here was a different culture altogether. The company—including *Seventeen* magazine and the *Daily Racing Form*—was sold for $3 billion by ultra-conservative American media mogul Walter Annenberg to ultra-conservative Australian media mogul Rupert Murdoch. While inside News Corp., I revived an idea I would have proposed at Time Inc. had I survived there: the *Parents' Guide to Children's Entertainment*. I suggested it once and was told no. I tried again; no again. Then one day an executive said,

"You know that magazine you want to start? Start it." OK, I answered, drawing on my magazine development experience at Time Inc. I'll write a proposal. No, he said, start it. Oh, good, I'll skip a step and produce a dummy for market research. No, he said again, exasperated, *start it. Launch it.* That was the company's seat-of-the-pants Aussie macho management style. No task forces and drunken lunches here. The problem was that the company was impatient for immediate winners and as we went to press I was told we would need to sell 1 million copies of the first issue with no promotion. It was printed *TV Guide*-size so it could fill slots at supermarket checkouts—until *TV Guide*'s circulation managers realized this was hurting their sales and the magazine was pulled after just two weeks on sale instead of two months. Still, we managed to sell 400,000 copies. They published a few more editions until *TV Guide*'s head of advertising sales said it just wasn't worth her time.

TV Guide had been a behemoth, at one time the most widely distributed and read weekly magazine in the country, indispensable next to clickers on couches from coast to coast. Beloved, collected, and highlighted in yellow marker by many, it was a cultural icon. It had a huge staff in suburban Philadelphia compiling previews and schedules for every show on every TV station. When cable came, it survived the competitive onslaught of Time Inc.'s *TV-Cable Week*. But *TV Guide* was a victim of the habit that sustained it. The editors wanted to provide complete cable listings but they couldn't fit everything on the *Guide*'s tiny pages. They wanted to produce the magazine on larger pages but the readers would not hear of it. Many prototypes were designed, many tests and focus groups held, many surveys sent. Nothing changed.

One year, the number of responses we received from our annual readers' survey was unusually low. That was odd, as *TV Guide*'s readers were the definition of loyal. A follow-up survey was conducted to see what happened; we learned that eighty percent of those who had not returned the survey had not done so because they had passed away. The readers were dying and the magazine was dying, just a little more slowly. I asked my boss, Anthea Disney, why we couldn't get the company to recognize the crisis. "You know why, Jeff," she said. "It's a cash cow." It was the cash cow in the coal mine, one of many once-gigantic magazines to shrink and fade. Magazines had become victims of their own success, unable to grow as they had in their pasts, unable to maintain their expectations of profitability, unable to reform in a changing media ecosystem. And then came the internet.

6 TANGLED IN THE WEB

I sat on a train eavesdropping as a stock broker tried to reel in his mark. "Have you heard of the internet?" he asked. "Rupert Murdoch just bought it." Not quite. In late 1993, News Corp. bought Delphi Internet, a tiny, dial-up online service that was, in fact, the first to offer plain folk—people outside of the military and universities—a gateway to get on the internet when it was still nothing more than monospaced characters on monochrome screens presenting menus of arcane applications, including gopher (a prehistoric web), archie (an ancient search engine), FTP (how we sent and retrieved documents), and IRC (early chat). I was TV critic at *TV Guide*, owned by News Corp., and in 1994 was headed to Cambridge, Massachusetts to take charge of Delphi's content. My wife and I put a down payment on a home and were a month from moving when I started.

I walked into a clusterfunk of epic proportion. Delphi was a charming little company of a few score wonderful, t-shirted nerds that was being invaded by Hollywood and New York media types in too-tight suits. The company's knowledgeable and avuncular CEO, Dan Bruns, was pushed aside so the company could be run, temporarily, by Murdoch's hanger-on brother-in-law, former Australian radio DJ Jaan Torv, with cameo appearances by the mogul's distracted son, James. The place was in a panic because Delphi did not have a GUI, a graphical user interface (pronounced "gooey"), like those that guided users through the sylvan, sanitized, and walled gardens of AOL, Prodigy, CompuServe, and GEnie. An oh-so-hip New York design firm with a reputation for making cool museum exhibits with much interactive button-pushing, Tom Nicholson Associates, was hired to build the GUI and I began attending meetings about the cartoon streetscapes and primary colors that News Corp.'s people thought would compete with the much-larger online services.

Mostly, the design meetings were about brands. News Corp., like every other media company about to tiptoe online, thought that what made them valuable in this new world was their brands. Those brands, they contended, represented trust, engagement, and value. One of the Hollywood types kept insisting that the most important job of a Delphi GUI was to direct users to News Corp. properties: magazines—*TV Guide, Seventeen, Mirabella* (a short-lived women's title); Fox TV shows—*The Simpsons, Beverly Hills, 90210*; and the company's movies. What would people get when they got to the brands? Promotion for the brands and their content: a navigational tautology, not so much a walled garden as a high hedgerow maze with no exit. I dared dissent.

I had come online the first time in 1981 when I bought an Osborne One computer—a hefty suitcase, it was the first "transportable" computer. I bought a modem so I could connect to CompuServe, where I was able to read news and, far better, talk with strangers about shared interests. Via my modem, I could also do so in bulletin boards and later on the usenet discussion groups, where I was enthralled to find devoted fans who compiled complete episode guides for most every series ever on TV. I started quoting them in my reviews. Thus I began to learn that the attraction of connection was conversation more than content. At GUI meetings in Nicholson's loft offices, I said just this. The nerds agreed; for them, brands were not the objects of public desire. The Hollywood folks ignored us; brands were everything.

Then, one day in my second week in Cambridge, one of the nerds showed off something new, called a web browser. Browsing was a word over which we editors had proprietary interest, for we believed magazines practically invented browsing. This browser was something very new. The nerd clicked on a blue "link" and showed how another "web page" from another "web site" appeared. The New York and Hollywood types shrugged; with all that h-t-t-p-colon-slash-slash shit, it was ugly and confusing, no place safe for brands. The nerds, however, quickly grasped the import of what they were seeing and, after they explained it to me, so did I. Up to this time, to be online meant choosing one or another service to dial into: AOL *or* CompuServe *or* Prodigy *or*, through Delphi, the incomprehensible internet. Now one could imagine linking from anything to anything in an open, networked world. The nerds realized that this was the end of the dial-up online service and the end of the GUI before Delphi even had one. The walls would fall.

A new boss arrived from IBM and announced he was going to move Delphi from Massachusetts to New York just as I was about to move from New York to Massachusetts. This boss was hired to side with Hollywood, not the nerds. By this time, I'd learned what a sinkhole the business was, as Delphi was spending almost $100 in marketing to acquire each new subscriber. I had to escape. After a month there, I called my former boss at the *San Francisco Examiner* and *New York Daily News*, Jim Willse, who was now working on online strategy for Advance Publications, publishers of newspapers across America, magazines at Condé Nast, and books at Random House. I begged for rescue and I am grateful he and the Newhouses took me in. It was from this perch that I was able to observe the struggle of every magazine and media company, including our own, to adjust to the internet and the web.

* * *

The Newhouses owned premier magazine brands: *Vogue, Glamour, Mademoiselle, Gourmet, Bon Appétit, Architectural Digest,* the *New Yorker, GQ, Vanity Fair, Brides,* and more. My boss, Steven Newhouse—son of Donald Newhouse and nephew of Si—certainly understood the value of magazine brands; they colored his blood. But he also understood their limitations. I'd watch Steve in meetings with online companies, including Yahoo and AOL, as they would salivate at the idea of snagging some *Vogue* content to shovel online. Steve gave them the silent treatment and side eye of a father unsure that he would ever give up his daughter to marriage with the likes of them. In truth, Steve believed magazine content was good for magazines, not so much for the internet. What was valuable online, he taught me, was the opportunity to connect people with each other about their interests and needs, their hobbies and neighborhoods, their kids' sports and their jobs, as I had done on CompuServe. Conversation over content. It was from Steve that I began to learn the value of what we would come to call interactivity: not pushing buttons in a museum but simply talking with other people by way of wires.

When I arrived, Newhouse and Willse were exploring which route Advance should take online: with many other publishers to the dumbed-down confines of Prodigy, or to the smaller but livelier AOL. Or there was this new thing, the web and the browser. Days after I started work at Advance, on October 13, 1994, Marc Andreessen released the first commercial, consumer browser, Netscape, to the market. That is the route we took.

The nascent business of the internet was hermaphroditic: like worms, nobody could figure out who was screwing whom, how. Online companies paid media companies for content but vowed that soon the tables would turn. "We're paying you now, but someday you will pay us," AOL executive

Ted Leonsis said to media people. Everybody debated who was a destination online and who was a portal—and what the hell a portal was—and which was more valuable to be. I cannot count how many times I sat through debates about whether content or distribution was king.

Magazine people thought the web was theirs to rule. "The metaphor that the Internet developed upon *sounded* like it was about publishing," Leonsis told John Motavalli in his book, *Bamboozled at the Revolution: How Big Media Lost Billions in the Battle for the Internet*. Leonsis recalled:

> Page views, browser, there was this manifest destiny that 'we' get it. The thought was that they wouldn't have called it a page view if it wasn't about publishing. Instead the Internet was really creating this new life form that wasn't about the traditional relationship between a reader and a publisher, or an advertiser and a reader. It was something new altogether.[1]

But magazine people insisted that the internet was just another medium, their medium, meant to serve their ends—namely, to carry their content, to sell subscriptions to their print publications, to place advertising from their clients, to promote their *brands*. They saw the web as—and an early venture took this name—the Electronic Newsstand.

* * *

In a dramedy with many acts, Time Warner was the laughingstock of the digital dawn. When it came to new media, the company was years past its lost fortune with *TV-Cable Week*. In December 1994, after much delay, Time Warner finally opened its much-touted Full Service Network cable service in five Florida homes, whose residents would be able to rent from fifty movies on demand, play games, and buy directly from Williams-Sonoma, Sharper Image, and, of course, the Warner Brothers store, featuring its brands. Time Warner CEO Gerald Levin declared: "The same kind of minds that denounced Galileo as a heretic, ridiculed Edison's notion of an electric powered light and dismissed the Wright brothers' ideas as a crackpot scheme have turned their sights on the new medium of interactivity. Interactivity is going to change how customers view the world."[2] To its credit, Time Warner was right about cable's future, only years too early. The Full Service Network closed after two and a half years at a reported loss of $100 million.

A few weeks earlier and eleven days after the release of Netscape Navigator, Time Inc. chose the American Magazine Conference to announce the unveiling of its home on the new web. Named after frontier novelist James Fenimore Cooper, Pathfinder was intended to guide people to the good stuff in this strange, new internet—that is, to Time Inc. brands. The *New York Times* reported:

> "We have every base covered now," Walter Isaacson, editor of new media at Time Inc., said. "We are going to have the best and the most ways to distribute our journalistic content to consumers, in any form they want—TV,

> on-line, CD-ROM, cable and, of course, our core business, print."
>
> Time Inc.'s new service, called Pathfinder, will be available to anyone with a computer, a modem, a software package called a browser and special access to the global web of computers known as the Internet. It will feature editorial content, including photographs and graphics, from Time, Vibe and Sunset magazines, as well as Time Warner Books.

The *Times* concluded its report with the words of a consultant at the conference who declared the internet "just the latest in a series of fads."[3]

In Pathfinder, Time Inc. revealed the worldview of every publisher. "They thought they would start Pathfinder as the next-generation online service where people would come into it and would never get out," a veteran of the venture, Chan Suh, told Motavalli. "So searching the Internet didn't make sense for them. Why would you want to search anything other than Time Warner content? Time Warner brings the world to you." Added Motavalli: "While virtually all media Web operations were guilty of this form of hubris, Time Inc.'s mistakes were greater simply because their hubris was more monumental and all-encompassing."[4]

Editors of the company's magazines were told they could not have their own stand-alone websites but had to subsume their digital ambitions and identities inside Pathfinder. Most editors at the time were dubious about putting any of their content and effort into the net, for they were paid to print not post it. Placing their content in a space they did not control? Well, that brought cries of cannibalization and passive resistance from editors and business executives. The magazine people and the web people never understood each other. "They put us in the basement for a reason: we techies didn't always fit well into the corporate culture at Time Inc.," recalled Marc Eliot Stein, one of those techies, writing in an online memoir of his time at the company. "Delegations from various parts of Time Warner would occasionally tour our basement cages and gape at us while we worked. Magazine people appeared to be particularly frightened of and fascinated by techies, and when we saw them watching we would perform tricks like eating Twinkies while typing."[5] One year after Pathfinder's debut, at the next annual American Magazine Conference, the newly appointed CEO of Time Inc. Don Logan (who headed the task force that had been assigned to find reasons to abort *Entertainment Weekly*), said of his company's website: "It's given new meaning to me of the scientific term black hole." Would this internet thing make money in the next five years? "To be perfectly honest," said Logan, "I don't have a clue."[6]

Five years after it began, Pathfinder was dead. An analyst recounted its many missteps for the *Times*: "'One of [those blunders] was burying all those wonderful consumer brands like Time magazine and Fortune magazine under the U.R.L. Pathfinder,' he said, referring to the Web address pathfinder .com."[7] After experiments with CD-ROMs and the Full

Service Network, dalliances with CompuServe and AOL, and now the folding of Pathfinder, Time Inc. had failed again. Time Inc. had a habit of buying the strategy it lacked. When it thought it was in the business of printing on paper, it bought a paper company, Temple Inland, which it later sold. When it was frightened by newcomer Chris Whittle publishing a series of magazines intended solely for doctors' waiting rooms—where the company gained much of its supposed public-place readership—Time Inc. spent $185 million to buy half the company in 1988. Whittle whittled through a fortune in magazines and a failed TV news channel beamed into school classrooms. It all faded away in ignominy. Time Warner had no strategy for the web, so it decided to merge with one. It made the worst merger in history, with AOL. The rest is infamy.

* * *

Time Inc. was by no means the only disaster-prone publishing company on the internet. Rupert Murdoch's catastrophes got less attention but were at least as numerous and as costly. In 1995 (after I'd escaped), News Corp. wrapped Delphi into what was to be a $1 billion venture with long-distance phone company MCI (just as the internet was about to make the idea of long-distance obsolete). Its minions labored in so-hip, loft-like New York offices building their version of Yahoo, a directory to the web called iGuide. Meanwhile, unbeknownst to News Corp., adulterous MCI was flirting with Time Inc. to merge instead with Pathfinder. Then MCI fell into bed with

Micrsoft to distribute its late-to-the-party browser, Internet Explorer. Only months after launching, iGuide died with nothing to show for the effort but untold millions lost. Three years after buying Delphi for a reported $15 million, News Corp. sold it back to Dan Bruns. Delphi Forums went on to become a company of online forums, of conversation; it lives still.

In 2005, Murdoch bought social media pioneer MySpace for $580 million. Two years later, I was invited to Murdoch's management retreat in Monterey, California to moderate a discussion with famously laconic Mark Zuckerberg and infamously inscrutable Nick Denton, founder of Gawker Media. On stage, we discussed the competing value of brands versus peers, new definitions of news (Zuckerberg had just dared to introduce the feature he called News Feed), and whether Denton's gossip blog might kill Murdoch's Page Six. More than once I saw Murdoch, still a fan of the internet, raise his hands to applaud something one of us said but, seeing no movement to do likewise from his dour executives, he dropped his hands silently into his lap. At the cocktail party that evening, a News Corp. executive asked Zuckerberg how old he was and he answered, "I'm *going to be* twenty-three." She thought that was just darling. At dinner, I sat across from Zuckerberg and Murdoch as the old mogul told the new one he should never sell his company. Zuckerberg was the first to leave Murdoch's party because his girlfriend wanted to see a movie. The minute he was gone, the founders of MySpace, who had been jealously watching their owner confer with their competitor from tables away, came rushing over to get Dad time.

At breakfast the next morning, Murdoch sat alone at a table, only his craggy brow visible over his copy of the *Wall Street Journal.* A few days later, he would buy the *Journal*'s parent company, Dow Jones, for $5 billion. A few years later, in 2011, he would sell MySpace for $35 million. He would waste about that much trying to start a newspaper for the iPad in 2011. That same year, he sold the IGN game network for an undisclosed loss; he'd bought it in 2005 for $650 million. As for *TV Guide*, its executives feared the business of TV listings would be superseded by a company called Gemstar, which held the patent for an algorithm that produced codes people could use to program VCRs to record shows. Gemstar merged with *TV Guide* and Murdoch bought controlling interest. The company was at one time worth $20 billion; he sold it for $2.8 billion to help pay for the purchase of the *Journal.* The print version of *TV Guide* was eventually unloaded for one dollar. Murdoch had been enamored of the internet and its young moguls but he would turn on it, using his publications to lobby against his new competitors, Google and Facebook.

Other magazine publishers around the world traveled a similar path from infatuation to jealous jilting. In Germany, magazine publisher Hubert Burda—proprietor of the popular magazines *Bunte, Focus*, and *Superillu*—was in love with the net, investing in cool startups and inviting the new moguls, including Zuckerberg, to speak at DLD, his annual, pre-Davos conference in wintery Munich. In 2009, I was on a panel about the future of media at that conference when Burda stood up to bewail the state of magazines online. “We all believed that there would be a good, profitable advertising model on the web. But it didn’t work,” he complained. The problem, he and other publishers discovered, was abundance. In print, Burda’s competition was “no more than two or three really good magazine companies in Germany. On the web you have these telcos, you have hundreds and hundreds of companies that bring your price down so you get lousy, lousy pennies on the web.” Thenceforth, whenever the internet was brought up in the company, the refrain “lousy, lousy pennies” was quick to follow, Burda’s equivalent of Time’s “black hole.”

* * *

At Condé Nast, Steve Newhouse understood that if the web were handed over to magazine or newspaper editors, they would shovel PDFs of their print pages onto the net and publishers would sell online ads as giveaways—“valued added”—alongside print. If that happened, media on the web would never explore its full potential nor establish its own economic value. So in magazines and newspapers both, the company set up new and independent digital companies. As at Time Inc. the legacy magazine editors had not been pleased and objected to “their content” being taken from their control. Unlike Time Inc. Condé Nast was not ruled by task forces but by the family who owned it. Thus the content was not the editors’ but Messrs. Newhouses’.

A wise and effulgent magazine creative director, Rochelle Udell, and my partner from *Entertainment Weekly*, Joan Feeney, set about building new websites around some of the magazines in a new division called CondéNet; I got to watch. Udell as president and Feeney as editor-in-chief began with Epicurious, a food site built with content from *Gourmet* and *Bon Appétit* and cookbooks from the then-Newhouse-owned Random House, in addition to many original features. Clearly, the ideal content for the service would be the decades' worth of the magazines' and books' recipes, but they existed only in archives, on paper. Because of the typographical arcanery of the form—lists of ingredients with fractions and abbreviations—optical character scanning was an impossibility. Every recipe had to be retyped into computers. Feeney found a squad of digital monks—yes, real monks—to do the work. According to her, much of the reason that Condé Nast tackled food was the belief that recipes were not subject to copyright as articles were, and writers' contracts at the time gave publishers permission to electronically reproduce their work only if it appeared in "facsimile form" (à la microfiche). Those contracts were all soon amended. Once the recipe database was up and working—giving users the opportunity to search on ingredients and more—Feeney and her team soon noted a huge spike in traffic every day at 4 p.m. when readers came home, searching on "chicken" to decide what to make for dinner. She called it "a humbling and helpful feedback loop."

Condé Nast had all the tools required to produce the monthly miracle that was a magazine but none of the skills needed to make a new-fangled website. At the time, consultants popped up like tulips in a bubble, so we hired a few. We hired a company called Open Market out of Cambridge, Massachusetts, which built websites and competed with Netscape in building server software for the new web. I remember a first meeting among its nerds and our editors. The geeks wanted a complete specification for every web page the editors would ever want. The editors, aghast, told the geeks to just start building and they would be told when they were close. It was then that I realized that magazines might not fit into the engineers' ecosystem of the net; this would be a clash of worldviews.

After starting Epicurious and a few online-only brands—one for dating, another for fitness—Feeney and company tackled the Mt. Everest of magazines, *Vogue*, ruled by the indomitable editor of editors, Anna Wintour. Feeney decided that the killer app, the equivalent to Epicurious' recipe database, had to be capturing every look on every model on every runway at the Paris, London, and New York fashion shows. This was audacious ambition, stretching the technological capabilities of the moment to the limit. Much negotiation ensued with the editors of each nations' *Vogues* and with the fashion shows, the designers (who had limited the number of pictures of looks allowed publications), and the models' agents and their unions. Digital photography was still new—Nikon released its first digital camera in

1986—and digital storage was infinitesimal by today's expectations. CondéNet hired photographers and rented truck trailers filled with computers and nerds and leased T1 telephone lines that would carry their photos at the fastest speed available: 1.5 megabytes per second. More important, Feeney and her team used the new capabilities technology provided to make this unprecedented collection of the collections searchable. The result was awe-inspiring: lush, beautiful, authoritative, useful, something no magazine could have ever made before, now possible thanks to the net.

Udell and Feeney built a formidable creative enterprise. Epicurious was immediately a darling of the infant web: elegant, tasteful, and actually useful. It was also truly interactive, to Newhouse's delight. Here again I saw the bounds of the magazine expand beyond content on pages. Under the recipes, users were permitted to leave comments and there they dared to suggest improvements to the high temples of taste. In Gail's Recipe Swap, a forum for readers to share recipes of their own, we witnessed the formation of a close community of food fanatics. I came to learn that the enthusiasm, expertise, and experience of the people formerly known as the audience—to borrow the phrase of New York University Professor Jay Rosen—was a valuable asset alongside the authoritative recipes from the bibles of food.

Newhouse and CondéNet pushed the limits again when they decided to create an online, high-end fashion store in Style.com. Feeney explained to expensive business consultants and investors that magazines had "always been in the business of creating demand, and now we could satisfy it with a click." As she recalled, "the suits always swooned." There was much concern over whether women would buy high-end fashion online. There was greater concern about whether designers would permit it. If anyone could convince haute couture to try, only Condé Nast and *Vogue* could. So a deal was made with high-echelon department store Neiman Marcus to handle logistics. Style.com would do the work of bringing in designers even Neiman Marcus could not sell and deciding what to offer. The site was beautiful, the fashion exquisite, the functionality functional. But come the online stock crash of 2000, Neiman Marcus could no longer stomach the risk, so the deal ended. To the shopper, nothing seemed to have changed; only the business model shifted: Instead of sharing a cut of sales and profits with Condé Nast, Neiman Marcus simply paid Style.com for advertising. Condé Nast reverted to form as merely media.

* * *

Advertising was supposed to support online media as it had offline. Around this time, I was appointed to join a stultifyingly boring committee of the Audit Bureau of Circulations, the body charged with verifying how many people paid for publications through subscriptions and newsstands. The ABC was grappling with what to do about the internet. Their assumption was that advertisers and their agencies would want a reliable third party to verify the size of a publication's audience, online as offline. So we spent unending, unbearable meetings arguing over much arcana, starting with the definition of a "page view." However, it soon became apparent that advertisers did not care about a website's total audience, only about the pages on which their own ads appeared and who saw them.

Then and there came the death of the Myth of Mass Media. Publishers could no longer claim that all readers saw all ads, charging all advertisers for all readers. This realization was the little-heralded mortal blow to the digital ambitions of magazine publishers and other legacy media online. Because publishers could not sell their total audiences to all their advertisers, they instead turned to manufacturing as many web pages of content as they could and ginning up audience for them through the new dark arts of search-engine optimization and social media—read: clickbait—attempting to eke out pennies for each ad each user saw. Now there was no scarcity of advertising competition—there was an infinite number of pages and page views across the web. That endless competition depressed the price of advertising, as abundance does.

As if that reality weren't difficult enough, Google came along and completely upended the economic model of advertising. If Google had operated like a publisher, it would have charged what the market would bear for a scarcity—e.g., how many people searched for "Paris" in a day. But instead of trying to control a scarcity, Google exploited the abundance of the web by placing ads everywhere. If your blog wrote about Paris restaurants, Google's content crawler could discern the topic of your page, place a Paris ad there if you wished, and share revenue with you. And there's more. First, advertisers paid only if a user clicked on their ads; thus Google shared risk with the advertiser, something publishers never did. Second, Google set the price of its advertising by auction, again lowering the value. Third, Google enabled the entry into the advertising market of countless small businesses that never before could have afforded expensive magazine ads, which meant that big advertisers had to be on Google to fight off their new competition. Publishers like to cry that Google stole their advertising. No, Google just changed the rules. Capitalism, baby.

Next, Google bought the ad platform DoubleClick, and advertising online was soon sold in huge, instantaneous, automated marketplaces based not on the brand of the publisher or the relevance of its content or the quality of its environment or the demographics of its audience but only on data: What do we know about each consumer? This is why, after you look at shoes online, those damned shoes will follow you all over the web as you look at sites that have nothing to do with shoes. It's the data point about your proclivity to purchase pumps that merchants want. Magazine content, audiences, and brands have been commodified. Thus, as Hubert Burda complained, publishers would end up with only lousy, lousy pennies. As a result, magazine publishers would soon follow newspaper publishers to retreat ever more behind paywalls.

The magazine industry never fully figured out the web. In fairness, neither did newspapers or television. By and large, old mass media kept looking for an ever-bigger mass. Most thought their value was in their content and their brands. They tried to convince advertisers that their websites were the place online to enhance those brands, but the brands learned they could now speak directly with their customers. Publishers failed to see that the internet abhors middlemen and they were middlemen.

Wikipedia maintains a list of defunct American print magazines, among them,

- *Gourmet* (1941–2009)
- *Mademoiselle* (1935–2001)
- *Premiere* (1987–2007)
- *U.S. News & World Report* (1933–2010)
- *Details* (1982–2015)
- *ESPN the Magazine* (1998–2019)
- *Mirabella* (1989–2000)
- *Business 2.0* (1995–2001)
- *George* (1995–2001)
- *Nickelodeon* (1990-2009)
- *Jane* (1997–2007)
- *Oui* (1964–2007)

- *Playboy* (1953–2020)
- *Playgirl* (1973–2016)

Some magazines are killed. Some magazines fade into self-parody, like *Forbes* and *Newsweek*. Some magazines—*New York, Elle, Cosmopolitan, Vogue, Vanity Fair*—reduce their frequency; *Entertainment Weekly* became a monthly (without changing its name) before going out of print. And some magazines supposedly go online. That was the fate of *EW* when it ceased publication in 2022 at Dotdash.

There have been printed rumors that even *People*, the most successful launch and once the most profitable magazine in America, could end its print run at Dotdash. Back when advertising was the profit center of print—the beneficiary of the Myth of Mass Media—publishers lost money on some subscribers because they made it up with ads. With ad revenue declining, the burden for supporting magazines fell back on readers. So Dotdash got rid of unprofitable readers, reducing the guaranteed circulations of some of its magazines: *Better Homes & Gardens* from 7 million to 4 million, *People* below 3.5 million, selling as few as 150,000 copies on newsstands, shocking for a magazine that once thrived there. "We are no longer willing to print magazines that people are no longer willing to pay for," Dotdash Meredith CEO Neil Vogel said. "We took a ton of revenue out of the print business because revenue isn't what's driving us now, it's brand and profitability." In a memo to staff, Vogel added: "We have said from the beginning, buying Meredith was about buying brands, not magazines or websites. It is not news to anyone that there has been a pronounced shift in readership and advertising from print to digital, and as a result, for a few important brands, print is no longer serving the brand's core purpose." *Brands.*

Vogel, however, declared print still alive. "The strategy: Moving forward, the company will invest in print products that cater to hyper-enthusiasts. We're actually going to add small pieces of print—not economically relevant—to some of our other brands."[8] Now, a century and a half after the industrialization of print, the mass is dead. Hyper-enthusiasts are the thing. In that sense, magazines—what is left of them—return to their origins, serving small audiences willing to pay for them.

It might be said that the internet's greatest challenge to magazines was not the abundance of content it generated, the endless competition for advertisers, or the constant struggle in merging material and virtual products, strategies, and cultures. The greatest challenge may turn out to be how the internet exposed the inexorably elite and isolated nature of the medium. At Condé Nast's *Bon Appétit*, a furor erupted when YouTube videos exposed how the magazine had been using people of color as "ethnic props" for diversity without giving them credit for their work and expertise, and also when an editor was caught wearing brownface. The *New York Times* called it a reckoning and the company's top executives, Wintour and the newly arrived CEO Roger Lynch, had to prostrate themselves in public.

Janice Min, a veteran editor of popular magazines, summed up Condé's pickle well when she said, "I think without the whiff of elitism, that sort of old-school top-down approach to telling the world what to wear and think, Condé Nast runs the risk of becoming just another white-label content farm on the web." Another, perish the thought, Dotdash factory. "How do you stay special and distinct and in a world that demands equity?" In other words, how can one serve the old, white, privileged classes, making them the center of culture, when voices too long not heard by or represented in haut monde media now speak loudly on Twitter, Facebook, YouTube, Instagram, and TikTok? It is there now that fashions are determined, stars are made, trends trend. Culture is not handed down from on high. Now the culture decides culture. The *Times*, hoping no doubt that the guillotine of digital self-determination would not fall on its aristocratic neck next, decreed that Condé had fallen from "the coolest place to the coldest one" and that "Condé Nast knows faded glory is not in style." The would-be journal of the educated proletariat, the *Nation*, gleefully chronicled the end of Condé's era, reviewing yet another book by another former Condé assistant: "Legends of elephantine expense accounts, personal drivers, boozy lunches, palace intrigue, and incessant starfucking: These are supposedly what made the gilded age of celebrity editors and their glossies great. Condé Nast was at the center of this lucre."[9]

Condé has backed away from the palace, leaving behind its Gehry-gewgawed lunchroom on Times Square for aseptic cubicles in One World Trade Center. Its latest CEO, Lynch, insists Condé is practically an organ of the masses, its 300 million readers on its websites and 450 million interactors on social media outnumbering its 70 million magazine readers. Said Lynch: "It's just that this is no longer a magazine company."[10] Condé is hardly the only company to retreat from ink on slick paper. The entire industry is withdrawing. In 2022, the News Media Alliance—formerly known as the Newspaper Association of America until the word "newspaper" presumed cobwebs—merged with their upmarket cousins of the Association of Magazine Media—formerly known as the Magazine Publishers Association until the word "publisher" took on an old-fashioned tone. Together, they adopted a new moniker with a modern slash: the News/Media Alliance. Almost three centuries after it was first put to use, the word "magazine" has lost its gloss.

7 NEXT

In 1960, Theodore H. White—a former *Time* correspondent who would win the Pulitzer Prize for *The Making of the President*—penned a roman à clef about the death of *Collier's* magazine, an event he had endured three years earlier. In *The View From the Fortieth Floor*, White dramatizes a once-great magazine empire's surrender to the sudden onslaught of television, the financialization of the media industry, and the commodification of the audience and its attention.

White has a rapacious financier in his tale explain magazine economics: "All I know is you price a copy at fifteen cents, you get back nine cents, and the goddam book costs us twenty, twenty-five, thirty cents to manufacture. So you lose fifteen, twenty cents every time you sell a copy. So you sell two hundred thousand more copies, we've lost another thirty, forty thousand bucks. Unless you get more advertising to pay the freight. And you ain't getting it." That was the business model invented by Frank Munsey in 1893, and this was the beginning of its end.

The story's hero, John Ridgely "call me Ridge" Warren, became the company's president and spent $2 million on direct-mail solicitations, goosing magazine circulation to compete with television for audience and advertising. "Truth and dreams get paid for these days by breakfast foods, by patent medicines, by cranberries, by under-armpit deodorants," Warren said. "And advertisers want an audience first, not the truth. I've got to make money first, then you can come in here and make speeches to me about truth or dreams or anything you want. That's my gamble."

The editors got the message and did their part, their moods rising and falling with reports of cover sales. "'Is God Worried?' was the lead cover-line on the current issue, and Warren winced, but it had sold." In an editorial meeting, one editor lectured another on the essence of their job:

> I'll tell you what you're fighting for, Foley, every single week, every single issue—to catch their attention and sell it. They've all got TV sets now, they've all got cars, radios, boats, houses, and gardens to dig in. They haven't got time to think or read. We're not even fighting for their dollars any more, they've all got change jingling in their pockets. We're fighting for their time—half an hour, quarter of an hour, five minutes of attention.

Having mortgaged the soul of the magazines for attention, the advertisers still went to TV. Bills for tons of paper came due. In the end, the magazines were worth more dead than alive, their subscription lists sold to a competitor, their presses pawned. On the last day, the newsroom was strung with black typewriter ribbons as funeral bunting.[1]

In writing this book, I have come to see how evanescent a magazine can be. Magazines have their time, which they tend to overstay before dying. Now the question is whether the magazine as an object has passed its day as well. That is their problem: that magazines see themselves as objects. Their materiality is their palace and now their prison.

The magazine is not a thing. As it slips the surly bonds of print, we can begin to see the magazine for what it was and could be: an institution. As an institution the magazine has fulfilled many roles: curator of the notable, nurturer of talent and art, cultural voice, polished mirror, distant observer, collected record of a time, national convener, community organizer, advocate and reformer, educator, aesthetic and literary model, entertainer, critic, birthplace of the mass market, arbiter of celebrity, fabricator of pathos and kitsch, prophet of trends, home for ideas, bulwark of institutions. Which of these is worth salvaging in new form and which is best left in its time? For this, it might help to examine the value of magazines in three arenas: writing and its impact, design and its influence, and finally community.

* * *

In his five-volume history of magazines, Frank Luther Mott categorized their import. First, "they provide a democratic literature" and "keep very close to their public." They are, in the words of one editor of *Scribner's Monthly*, "the intellectual food of the people." Second, they support literature, printing leading authors and paying for their creation. "In belles-lettres at least," wrote William Dean Howells of the *Atlantic* and *Harper's* at their heights, "most of the best literature now sees the light in the magazines, and most of the second-best appears first in book form." Third, magazines "furnish an invaluable contemporaneous history of their times." To study magazines, said Mott, is to study "the thoughts and feelings of the people, the development of their taste in art and music and letters, their daily work and play, and even their fads."[2]

Frederick Lewis Allen was an editor at each of the three citadels of intellectual periodical print, at the *Atlantic* from 1914, the *Century* from 1916, then *Harper's*, where he became editor-in-chief in 1941. Writing in a fourth, *Scribner's Magazine,* on the occasion of its fiftieth anniversary, Allen distilled the media genre to its aspirational essence:

> It represented a valid ideal: the ideal of the educated man, the philosopher, who is at home not merely in his own land and his own age, but in all lands and all ages; from whose point of perspective the Babylonian seal-workers are as interesting as the Pittsburgh steelworkers; who lives not merely in the world of food and drink and shelter and business and politics and everyday commonplace, but in the timeless world of ideas.[3]

What has the magazine become? Take that once-august pillar of New England literature and culture, the *Atlantic.* On the one hand, it supports some of the finest reporting in print and online today, most notably by Ed Yong, brilliant reporter and explainer of science and medicine in the pandemic. But it can also be a lava flow of hot takes, falling over itself to plug into the contrarian zeitgeist before Vox or a hundred Substack newsletters or a corral of *New York Times* guest essayists can beat them to it: "Have Smartphones Destroyed a Generation?" "Facebook is a Doomsday Machine" "How the Enlightenment Ends." It has become at once an exemplar and a self-parody of the form. Like many magazines, the *Atlantic* decided the best way to address the onslaught of abundance of voices and viewpoints on the internet was with abundance of its own, hiring more writers and launching more newsletters and podcasts. Thereby it misinterprets the essence of the magazine: not abundance but exquisitely contained scarcity of space, time, ideas, talent, quality, and judgment.

In the overflow of speech online, I grant there is much to mourn: the epidemic credulity, disinformation, idiocy, lies, and bigotry, which were always lurking at the corner of the bar but are now bared and blared for all to hear. Yet we must keep in mind that amid the net's cacophony are voices too long not heard, represented, or respected in mass media, especially in magazines. Among them are unseen talents, unique perspectives forged from experiences outside media's elite worldviews, and unorthodox genres of expression. If we stand back and ask what we need in this new ecosystem of speech and creativity at scale, it is not to pile more talk upon talk. What we need is someone or something to take on the role that *Harper's Monthly* set out for itself on the first page of its first issue, "to place within the reach of the great mass of the American people the unbounded treasures of the Periodical Literature of the present day."[4]

Media have lately and largely dismissed what they think of as the content of the internet, calling it the gutter and worse. They are jealous of the internet's success amid their failure. They can be snobs. But imagine if a modern *Harper's* were to go to the effort to reach into the vastness of the net to find that which is worthy of attention. What a service that could be. I envision that modern editor listening for people who are authoritative, expert, artful, diverse in experience and viewpoint. I don't know what the end result might look like. As Jared Gardner characterized the early American magazine, it was

> premised on the notion that through proper arrangement multiple voices might be experienced not as cacophonous but as productive of further conversation and of the entrance into the field of new voices. It was premised on the belief that seemingly unrelated topics and agendas might be judiciously placed side by side so as to produce new fields of inquiry and new correspondences previously unimagined. It was one that refused the binaries of political parties, of American vs. British, of original vs. imitative, and of author vs. reader. It was, in short, premised on a profound confidence—bordering at times on utopianism—that the literary commons imagined

by the early American magazine might provide the machinery for a new model of collaborative citizenship.[5]

The early magazine was a vital cultural tool, nurturing fine writing, fiction, and a new, American voice. In the *Atlantic*, Howells acted as editor, critic, and writer, promoting a school of realism in fiction, and providing a blueprint for it in his novel about starting a magazine, *A Hazard of New Fortunes*. Fiction, Howells decreed, must reflect life. Frank Munsey instead promoted the virtue in romanticism as he launched the first all-fiction magazine, *Golden Argosy*. "These are the days when the romantic in literature—the strong, the shining, the imaginative, the ennobling—flourishes and holds the ear of the world," said *Munsey's*, "while 'realism' and 'veritism' are the languishing cults of the select few."[6] Culture war is a cheap and meaningless term today but in a real sense, magazines of the time, both high and low, fought to determine the course of American arts through their fiction.

The roster of novelists whose work received support in magazines is long and honorable (if hardly diverse): Robert Louis Stevenson, Stephen Crane, Harriet Beecher Stowe, Ernest Hemingway, Willa Cather, Joseph Conrad, Edith Wharton, Sinclair Lewis, William Faulkner. Book publishers—Harper, Putnam, Scribner—founded magazines to promote their authors' work. Book editors offered serial rights to magazine editors to tout their stories. Some magazines printed entire novels in their pages. Fiction was a staple, a draw in magazines of all genres—literary, intellectual, women's, children's, science fiction, pulp—for about a century.

And then, suddenly it seemed, fiction all but disappeared from periodical print. Yes, the surviving grand dames, *Harper's* and the *Atlantic*, plus their little sibling, the *New Yorker*, still run short stories, for old time's sake. But pity the would-be writer poring over *Writer's Market* to find a home for her coming-of-age tale. Mourn, too, the poet. Magazines helped writers strop their pens and, not insignificantly, helped pay bills as they worked on books. Why did magazine fiction die? Some blame cheap paperbacks, others television, where we more than sate our desire for drama, tragedy, and comedy. Who will nurture the best of writing— of creativity—now?

* * *

Magazines have been, since soon after their birth, a visual as much as a textual medium. They established the art and industry of illustration. Then, following the next hot thing, they embraced photography. Now, with the decline of magazines and of photo editors' budgets, photographers have fewer avenues of support for their work. And beware the impact AI-generated art will have on illustration and media. Still, with photography at the heart of the very visual web, I do not so much worry about the fate of the photo.

It's the fate of design that I fret over. The web is butt ugly. Like many a baby, it was born that way—with its color scheme of neon blue links against Navy-gray background, its atrocious sense of typography, its fuzzy photos and seizure-inducing dancing GIFs. Then media companies made it even worse. Their sites are slow and irritating. They interrupt the flow of text with animated ads and promotional (instead of contextual) links. They insert any handy and often irrelevant image. The web to date—apart from perhaps medium—lacks any sense of typography. Thus it lacks visual impact. The problem might be the absence of the artistic boundaries the paper page imposed. Or it could be the lack of a sense of posterity in a medium that has no memory. Or is it greed, the need to suck every second and penny possible from a promiscuous transaction with the person formerly known as the reader, now the user?

Think back to the work of Walter Bernard and Milton Glaser when they, with editor Clay Felker, created a distinct visual voice for news in *New York Magazine,* which they recount in their book *Mag Men*. At its launch, as a supplement in the *New York Herald-Tribune* and short-lived *New York World Journal Tribune*, it did not need to seduce the newspaper reader into picking it up and buying it; it was a Sunday bonus. Once orphaned onto the newsstand, the magazine quickly developed a *New York* visual attitude with bold, funny, savvy, self-aware, and compelling illustrations and photography. It turned pizzas and pastrami sandwiches into *objets d'arts* in infographics for the Underground Gourmet. It used fists and bolts of lightning as symbols of power in their city. Its caricatures of Richard Nixon were many and mean. Its photography could be as gritty as the city it portrayed. Every magazine had its unique and instantly recognizable style. Another brilliant editor, Adam Moss, carried on their tradition when he took the helm at *New York* after the unfortunate folding of his bold and surprising city magazine, *7 Days*.

As long as I've been alive and buying magazines, there was nothing more delightful than browsing the beautiful, staggering, informative, and memorable pages designed for *New York*, *Vogue*, *Gourmet*, *Esquire*, *Vanity Fair*, *Spy*, *Evergreen Review*, *Fortune*, *Life*, and on and on. Online, browsing is no longer an enviable luxury but a network time waster.

It wasn't just editorial designers who set the cultural aesthetic. It was first the advertisers. Once freed from the constraints of newspapers' agate type in single columns, marketers luxuriated in the white space, sizable illustrations, strong typography, hospitable environment, and bold branding of the magazine page. No one made better use of white space than Volkswagen, with its tiny car and witty text block. Absolut sculpted art from life in the shape of a vodka bottle. Who didn't love "You don't have to be Jewish to love Levy's real Jewish rye" or "Got milk?" Creative directors at ad agencies made memes before we could imagine what a meme would be; every visual we see on Twitter or Instagram is just a form of advertisement for an idea.

And magazine advertisements, in some ways more than the editorial, preserved the zeitgeist of their time: Black women cooking as a statement of continued servitude; family tableaux more idealized than any sitcom or sermon;

women smoking as a statement of alleged liberation. The advertisers gave the editors permission to be brassy because the advertisers had to be ever more startling to stand out as editors played catch-up. Together, designers on both sides of the magazine wall between editorial and advertising advanced the contemporary art, I say, more than the designers of cars, fashion, furniture, or architecture. But today, editors and advertisers alike trash the web.

* * *

To me, the essence of the magazine is neither text nor illustration but community.

In the early days of the web, I was asked to speak at a magazine conference because I was known to blog polemical pronouncements about the fate of print media if they did not wise up to the reality of the internet. The organizer and I agreed to the date and time and then, before ending our call, he asked, "But Jeff, are you going to say that magazines are doomed? And if you are, could you not come?"

I didn't say that magazines were doomed. To the contrary, I declared that magazines should be the best positioned genre of media to not only survive but prosper in the connected age. For magazines, whether they knew it and liked it or not, were built upon community. Magazines were maypoles around which readers gathered because they shared an interest, a need, a circumstance, a particular cultural taste and predilection, an affinity . . . a community, albeit imagined. The magazine set the idea of community free from the bonds of geography and wove people together across the new nation. In 1779, the *United States Magazine* celebrated the idea that "the mechanic of the city, or the husbandman who ploughs his farm by the river's bank" could become a magistrate or fill a seat in the Continental Congress. "This happy circumstance lays an obligation upon every individual to exert a double industry to qualify himself for the great trust which may, one day, be reposed in him. It becomes him to obtain some knowledge of the history and principles of government, or at least to understand the policy and commerce of his own country." How might he do that? Well, of course, by reading this magazine "that will in itself contain a library, and be the literary coffee-house of public conversation."[7]

Farmers, Presbyterians, and even spelling reformers (publishers of the *Fonetic Advocate* and *Fonetic Propagandist*) each had their own periodicals to give them common grounding. "Magazines and readers mutually construct communal identities," said Heather Haveman. "They are the social glue that brings together people who would otherwise never meet face-to-face, allowing readers to receive and react to the same cultural messages at the same time and, in many cases, encouraging readers to contribute to shared cultural projects."[8] Magazines at first sought to tie the new nation together; later they could be accused of dividing the nation as they served readers affiliated with separate religions, social-reform movements, or interests. In either case, magazines fostered a sense of belonging.

The sociologist William Kornhauser has theorized that the key to avoiding the perils of totalitarian or mass society is to foster pluralistic society, marked by belonging to clubs, congregations, and organizations so as to counter the power of the leader or the mob. Now more than ever, we need devices to foster that sense of connection that magazines once nurtured.

Magazines, I preached to that long-ago conference, should have been the first to use all the social tools of the internet to gather, connect, converse with, and serve the communities they already convened. Said Mark Harris of *Entertainment Weekly*: "We were writing for the entertainment obsessive across the country and that person really felt like reading the magazine at its best was like walking through a door into a club of welcoming, like-minded people." Precisely. But editors did not wish to see themselves as scout troop leaders or party hostesses or pastors. They were manufacturers of content. They were gatekeepers. They were agenda-setters. They thought people wanted to gather around editors and writers and what they made. When editors spoke of community they envisioned their own fan clubs. If they made any concession to conversation, it was to allow readers to comment on the content the magazines made: letters in print, comments online. Having paid no attention to those comments and offering no moderation, these forums inevitably slid into the sewer, allowing the editors to say: "See, told you, they're all idiots and jerks." Which is a helluva way to view one's own community.

Thus magazines made what would turn out to be their fatal mistake. They could have beat AOL, Reddit, Tumblr, Facebook, and Twitter to the punch as homes for conversation and community. A few tried. When Feeney and her colleagues started the Gail's Recipe Swap at Epicurious, the conversationalists there became so much a community that they arranged their own in-person meetups from across the country; they held CondéNet hostage and threatened to take their coffee klatches elsewhere unless it provided chat software; and they demanded that it open a separate forum where they organized their own project in regional recipes. From that I learned that it wasn't up to us to lead the users; given half a chance, the right tools, and enough respect, they would lead us.

In their day, magazines led. They did not just gather communities; they moved communities to action in campaigns and crusades. Magazines were prime movers in the holy war to abolish slavery. Harriet Beecher Stowe's *Uncle Tom's Cabin* was published first in forty installments in the abolitionist Washington weekly the *National Era*. "Thus," said Haveman, "the development of magazines was a cause, not merely a consequence or companion, of the growth of anti-slavery organizations."[9] Magazines lobbied for prohibition, vegetarianism, universal observance of the Sabbath, and unions, and against war and capital punishment. Generations later, *Playboy*, sexist objectification and all, played its part in America's sexual awakening. In recompense, Gloria Steinem's *Ms. Magazine*, a spinoff from *New York*, became a journal of feminism. Growing up in the sixties, I was radicalized about the Vietnam War in great measure by *Ramparts*, not to mention the *Nation*, *Rolling Stone*, and untold underground publications and mimeographed zines. Today, there is a crying need for such leadership. Not memes, not hot takes, not performative use of hashtags, but leadership.

Where are the media that do not merely comment on but map a path to defeat the fascist right-wing organizing across the neighborhood fence? Where is the media-led campaign to win back voting rights for all citizens, the crusade for the climate, the war to protect women's province over their bodies, the clarion call for racial reparations? If we see such advocacy anywhere in media, it is in Black, Latino, LGBTQ, and other outlets and in emergent communities lashed together on social media. In the early days of magazines and America, publications were launched with the explicit aim of defining a nation and rallying citizens around a vision for it. Instead, today, we are trapped in the both-sidesing of contemporary American journalism, amplifying and normalizing extremes so as to set the journalist's compass in the mythical center, the world revolving around them.

Perhaps I dream too much, wishing for the evolution of the magazine and its values in this new reality. Perhaps instead this is the end of the line for the magazine. The magazine is an object of its zeitgeist. No magazine is meant to live forever. *Entertainment Weekly* was destined for a brief slice of time when media choice was just exploding. It does not belong in a time when anyone can be an entertainer and everyone a critic. It could not adapt to YouTube and Reddit and TikTok. It fulfilled its purpose and, though my baby, I will judge that it hung on too long, as magazines do.

Step back in time. *Life* magazine was the world's mirror, or so it presented itself, first in black-and-white, then color through its three and a half tumultuous decades. *Life* made photos stories. It made photographers—Margaret Bourke-White, Gordon Parks, Alfred Eisenstaedt—auteurs. It presented an anodyne America—movie stars, wonders of the human body, heartfelt human interest—but also life's grit—war, poverty, racism. Dick Stolley legendarily negotiated to acquire the Zapruder film of John F. Kennedy's assassination, nine of its frames blown up over two oversize *Life* pages in images that are etched into the memories of any American alive then. It was thus the precursor to witness video shot on phones and shared online. *Life* was television before television. But then came television, whose images moved and spoke, making *Life* obsolete. After more than one attempt to resurrect it, *Life* lives on like a propped up cadaver to lend its red-boxed brand to special issues of cultural pap on the Barnes & Noble stand: *Cats: Companions in Life; Remembering Elvis Presley: The King Lives on; Jaws: The Shark Movie that Changed the World; History of the Rifle: The Weapon that Changed the World; Dogs: Why We Need Them. Why They Need Us.*

Farther back in time, *National Geographic* was the chronicle of the last age of discovery, before everything that was to be seen was seen. It documented wondrous, alien sights: people, animals, cultures, landscapes that only the intrepid explorer could have witnessed before. It took us around the world and mapped our journeys. What school child did not pore over its pages to the approval of parents and teachers, even with naked breasts, which didn't count because they were from far away? So many thought *National Geographic* was an object to be saved for the ages, though collections are now for sale for cheap in used bookstores, heirs finding them even less valuable than Grandma's silver and her Hummel figurines. NatGeo tried to get with the times, producing CD-ROMs and TV shows and a cable channel that ended up under the control of Rupert Murdoch and then Disney, and that's what has massacred the brand, cheapening it with shark weeks and so-called reality TV and too much Hitler. It might be better off extinct.

They each fulfilled their roles. Magazines, each in their time, captured the will and wish of their age in amber—or perhaps just aspic. Now, everyone is media: authors of blog posts, tweets, podcasts, Facebook posts, Instagram memes, TikTok duets, or snarky comments. What Montaigne let loose can no longer be contained by the press. The business justification of the magazine in its last, long century—the mass market—is dying, mortally wounded by internet connection and commerce, data and globalization. The cultural rationale of the magazine is challenged by people who now speak for themselves, not as archetypes—characters in writers' narratives. There is no myth of unity possible when the voices of the public are no longer constrained to opinion polls or a random quote fulfilling a writer's storyline. Now everyone can be heard in the cacophony we must learn to accept as the sound of democracy, good and bad. The essential myth of the magazine—that a culture can be encased or directed in so many regularly published pages—is punctured, gone. This, then, is an elegy for the magazine as object and subject of society.

NOTES

Chapter 1

1 For more, see the Museum of Radiation and Radioactivity on glossy paper: https://www.orau.org/health-physics-museum/collection/consumer/miscellaneous/glossy-paper.html

Chapter 2

1 *Seinfeld*, "The Cigar Store Indian," season 5, episode 10, Dec. 9, 1993.

2 Petersen.

3 Petersen.

Chapter 3

1 "Reading a newspaper is like reading a novel whose author has abandoned any thought of a coherent plot," said Benedict Anderson in a footnote in *Imagined Communities*, Verso, 2006, 10.

2 Jürgen Habermas, "Reflections and Hypotheses on a Further Structural Transformation of the Political Public Sphere," *Theory, Culture & Society*, Vol. 39, no. 4, Sept. 5, 2022.

3 Addison in *Addison and Steele: Selections From the Tatler and the Spectator*, Herbert Vaughan Abbot, editor, Scott Foresman, 1914, 52.

4 Samuel Johnson, Lives of the English Poets, n.p.

5 Gardner, 42.

6 Ellis, 172-175, 223-225.

7 Samuel Johnson, *The Gentleman's Magazine*, Preface, Vol. 10, 1740, iv.

8 Gardner, 55.

9 David A. Brewer, *The Afterlife of Character, 1726-1825*, University of Pennsylvania Press, 2005.

10 Iona Italia, *The Rise of Literary Journalism in the Eighteenth Century*, Taylor & Francis, 2005, 110-113.

11 Attributed to Samuel Johnson, "An Account of the Life of the Late Mr Edward Cave," *The Gentleman's Magazine*, Feb. 1754, 57.

12 J.A. Leo Lemay, *The Life of Benjamin Franklin*, Volume 2, University of Pennsylvania Press, 2006, 299-309.

13 Gary Coll, "Noah Webster: Journalist, 1783-1803." Dissertation, Southern Illinois University, 1971, 98.

14 Gardner, 69-76.

15 Coll, 107-108.

16 Webster, *American Magazine*, February 1788.

17 Haveman 9, 25-26, 29.

18 Quoted in Mott, Vol. 1, 194.

19 Tebbel, 6, 10.

20 Gardner, 3.

21 Illinois Monthly Magazine, April 1831, 302.

22 Haveman, 30; Tebbel, 39.

23 Mott Vol. 1, 351, 580-594.

24 Mott Vol. 1, 591; *Godey's Lady's Book* Jan. 1852, 93, and an advertisement, 1850.

25 *Putnam's Monthly*, March 1857, 293-296.

26 Mott, Vol. 3, 17.

Chapter 4

1 Britt, 2, 4, 13.

2 Munsey, 39-40.

3 Munsey, 38-40.

4 Ohmann, 82, 101.

5 McClure, 243-244.

6 William Archer, *The Fortnightly Review,* 1910, 921-932.

7 Mencken, First Series, 171-180.

8 Ohmann, 221.

9 Mott Vol. IV, 10.

10 John H. Johnson, "The Untold Story of How Publisher Made Millions With a $500 Loan," *Ebony*, June 1989, 48-53.

11 For more, see the NAACP's history: https://naacp.org/find-resources/history-explained/history-crisis

12 Johnson, *Succeeding Against the Odds*, 156.

13 Brown, 35, 39, 48-49, 6, 5, 7.

14 Comstock quoted in Sohn, 33.

15 Mencken quoted in Eric Longley, "Mencken vs. the Post Office," *Menckeniana* 140, Winter 1996, 7; and in Corn-Revere, 59.

16 Mencken, Fifth Series, 15.

17 Time prospectus quoted in Mott, Vol 5, 295-296.

18 Luce quoted in Brinkley, 108-109.

19 Dwight Macdonald, *The Nation*, May 1 and 22, 1937; Marshall McLuhan, *Mechanical Bride,* Beacon Press, 1967, 10-11.

Chapter 5

1 Joseph Epstein, "Henry Luce & His Time," *Commentary*, November 1967.

Chapter 6

1 Motavalli, 122, 33.

2 "The Multimedia Project—Orlando/Florida." *Medienwissenschaft*, vol. 3. Teilband, Walter de Gruyter, 2002, https://doi.org/10.1515/9783110166767.3.50.2213.

3 Diedre Carmondy, *The New York Times*, Oct. 24, 1994, section D, 10.

4 Motavalli, 71.

5 Marc Eliot Stein, "Chapter 11: In the Pathfinder Basement," Literary Kicks, April 2, 2009. https://litkicks.com/inthepathfinderbasement/

6 Carmondy, *The New York Times*, Nov. 13, 1995, section D, 7.

7 Alex Kuczynski, *The New York Times*, April 27, 1999, section C, 1.

8 Sara Fischer, "Exclusive: Dotdash Meredith targeting print investments," Axios, May 31, 2022, https://www.axios.com/2022/05/31/exclusive-dotdash-meredith-targeting-print-investments. Alexandra Steigrad, "People's print magazine faces possible closure amid newsroom chaos," *New York Post*, May 16, 2022, https://nypost.com/2022/05/16/peoples-print-magazine-faces-closure-sources/.

9 Lozano, Kevin, "A Gilded Age," *The Nation*, July 12, 2022.

10 https://www.nytimes.com/2022/05/23/opinion/sway-kara-swisher-roger-lynch.html?showTranscript=1, https://www.nytimes.com/2022/05/10/books/magazine-industry-memoirs-anna-wintour-dana-brown.html?action=click&module=Well&pgtype=Homepage&section=Books

Chapter 7

1 White, 12, 35, 78, 459. He sold movie rights for the book to Gary Cooper, who died of cancer months later; the movie was never made. But the payment allowed White to pursue his series of books on presidential campaigns.

2 Mott, Vol. 1, 2-4.

3 Frederick Lewis, *Scribner's Magazine*, January 1937, 19-24. Note that *Scribner's Monthly* became *The Century* when

Scribner's publishing house sold it. Years later, the publishing house developed seller's remorse, and so it started *Scribner's Magazine*.

4 Harper's New Monthly Magazine, No. 1, June, 1850, p. 1.

5 Gardner, 172.

6 *Munsey's* in 1894, quoted in Tebbell, 74.

7 *The United States Magazine*, Jan. 1779, 9.

8 Haveman, 5.

9 Haveman, 20.

BIBLIOGRAPHY

Bernard, Walter and Milton Glaser. *Mag Men: Fifty Years of Making Magazines*. Columbia University Press, 2019.

Brinkley, Alan. *The Publisher: Henry Luce and His American Century*. Knopf, 2010.

Britt, George. *Forty Years—Forty Millions: The Career of Frank A. Munsey*. Kennikat Press, 1972.

Brown, Korey Bowers. *Souled Out:* Ebony *Magazine in an Age of Black Power, 1965–1975*. Dissertation, Howard University, 2010.

Byron, Christopher. *The Fanciest Dive*. Norton, 1986

Corn-Revere, Robert. *The Mind of the Censor and the Eye of the Beholder: The First Amendment and the Censor's Dilemma*. Cambridge, 2021.

Aytoun Ellis, *The Penny Universities*. Secker & Warburg, 1956.

Elson, Robert T. *Time Inc.: The Intimate History of a Publishing Enterprise, 1923–1941*. Atheneum, 1968.

Elson, Robert T. *Time Inc.: The Intimate History of a Publishing Enterprise, Volume 2, 1941-1960*. Atheneum, 1973.

Gardner, Jared. *The Rise and Fall of Early American Magazine Culture*. University of Illinois Press, 2014.

Gorton, Stephanie. *Citizen Reporters: S.S. McClure, Ida Tarbell, and the Magazine that Rewrote America*. Ecco, 2020.

Haveman, Heather A. *Magazines and the Making of America*. Princeton University Press, 2020.

Johnson, John H. *Succeeding Against the Odds: The Autobiography of a Great American Businessman*. Amistad, 1992.

McClure, S.S. *My Autobiography*. Frederick A. Stokes, 1914.
Mencken, Henry Louis. *Prejudices*, First and Fifth Series. Knopf, 1921, 1926.
Motavalli, John. *Bamboozled at the Revolution: How Big Media Lost Billions in the Battle for the Internet*. Viking, 2002.
Mott, Frank Luther. *A History of American Magazines: 1741–1850*. Vol. 1. D. Appleton and Company, 1930.
Mott, Frank Luther. *A History of American Magazines, 1850–1865*. Vol. 2. Harvard University Press, 1938.
Mott, Frank Luther. *A History of American Magazines, 1865–1885*. Vol. 3. Harvard University Press, 1938.
Mott, Frank Luther. *A History of American Magazines, 1885–1905*. Vol. 4. Belknap Press, 1957.
Mott, Frank Luther. *A History of American Magazines: Sketches of 21 Magazines, 1905–1930*. Vol. 5. Belknap Press, 1968.
Munsey, Frank A. *The Founding of the Munsey Publishing-House*. De Vinne Press, 1907.
Ohmann, Richard Malin. *Selling Culture*. Verso, 1996.
Petersen, Anne Helen. "The Trials of 'Entertainment Weekly': One Magazine's 24 Years of Corporate Torture." *The Awl*, theawl.com/2014/06/the-trials-of-entertainment-weekly-one-magazines-24-years-of-corporate-torture/.
Prendergast, Curtis and Geoffrey Colvin. *The World of Time Inc.: The Intimate History of a Changing Enterprise, 1960–1980*. Atheneum, 1986.
Sohn, Amy. *The Man Who Hated Women: Sex, Censorship, & Civil Liberties in the Gilded Age*, FSG, 2021.
Sumner, David E. *The Magazine Century: American Magazines Since 1900*. Peter Lang, 2010.
Tebbel, John William, and Mary Ellen Zuckerman. *The Magazine in America, 1741–1990*. Oxford University Press, 1991.
White, Theodore H. *The View from the Fortieth Floor*. Sloane, 1960.

INDEX

Addison, Joseph 3, 44–7 *see also Tatler*
Advance Publications 40, 86–7, 94–5
advertising
  advertisers 2, 4, 8, 16, 22, 37
  in print 19, 124–25, 63–5, 115, 124–25
  online 96, 103, 107–12
  see also clickbait, Myth of Mass Media
AOL 6, 28, 92–3, 95, 100, 128
Archer, William 66–7 *see also Fortnightly Review*
Atlantic, the (magazine) 4–5, 49, 59, 63, 68, 81, 118–19, 121–22

blogs 46, 101, 109, 125, 131
Bon Appetit 56, 86, 94, 104, 112
Bradford, Andrew *see American Magazine*
Brother Jonathan (magazine) 57 *see also* fiction in magazines
business model of magazines 22–28, 37–8, 61–5, 68, 71, 115

cable television 14, 16–18, 77, 88, 98, 131 *see also TV-Cable Week*
capitalism 7, 76, 109
Cave, Edward 3, 47–9, 55 *see also Gentleman's Magazine*
celebrity 4, 10, 14, 23, 55, 68–70, 76, 81, 113, 117
class culture in magazines 19, 63–4, 67–8 *see also* celebrity
clickbait 10, 108 *see also* advertising

Comstock, Anthony 71–2 *see also* US Postal Service
Condé Nast 2, 7, 40, 84–6, 94, 103–107, 112–13 *see also* CondéNet
CondéNet 104–106, 128
copyright law 48, 50
Cosmopolitan (magazine) 63, 87, 111
culture of magazines 85–7, 99

defunct American magazines, list of 110–111
dial-up internet 91–4
dime magazines 63, 66–7
DotDash Meredith 7, 111, 113
Du Bois, W.E.B. *see Negro Digest*

Ebony (magazine) 69–71
Economist, the (magazine) 2, 50, 81
Entertainment Weekly
  critics of 35–6
  end of 33, 40–1, 99, 111
  founding of 6–7, 15–22
  launch 23–7
  misfit status 29, 35, 82
  see also Time Inc.
Epicurious (online magazine) 104–106, 128

Feeney, Joan 29–30, 33, 38–40, 83–4, 104–107, 128 *see also* Epicurious
fiction in magazines 4, 31, 52–5, 57, 59, 62, 72, 121–22 *see also Brother Jonathan* (magazine); *Harper's New Monthly Magazine*; *New Yorker* (magazine)
Franklin, Benjamin 3, 48–50 *see also General Magazine*
Full Service Network *see* Time Warner

Gardner, Jared 45, 48, 50, 52, 120
gatekeeping 4, 15, 127
Gentleman's Magazine 3, 47–50
Google 102, 108–109
graphical user interfaces (GUIs) 92–4 *see also* dial-up internet
group journalism 81–5

Habermas, Jürgen 44–5
Hadden, Briton *see Time* (magazine)
Harper's New Monthly Magazine 4–5, 56–9, 62–4, 81, 97, 118–22
Harris, Mark 31, 19, 127

illustrations in magazines 2, 55–6, 62, 64, 122–25

Jarvis, Jeff 35, 38–9, 79–8
Johnson, John H. 69–70 *see also Ebony*
Johnson, Samuel 45, 47, 48 *see also Gentleman's Magazine*

legacy magazine companies *see* DotDash Meredith, Time Inc., Time Warner
Life (magazine) 29, 71, 76, 124, 130
Luce, Henry 16, 73–4, 76–7, 81 *see also Sports Illustrated; Time* (magazine)
Luther Mott, Frank 53–5, 58–9, 68, 117–18

magazines
  for abolition 54, 58 *see also* Du Bois, W.E.B
  for women 54–5
  progressivism 54, 58, 128–29
McClure, S.S. 63, 65–8 *see also McClure's* (magazine)
McClure's (magazine) 65–6, 68
McManus, Jason 20, 34, 36, 38, 40
Munsey, Frank 62–5, 72, 115, 121 *see also Munsey's* (magazine)
Munsey's (magazine) 62, 67–8
Murdoch, Rupert 87, 91–2, 100–102, 131
Myth of Mass Media 25, 108–112

National Geographic (magazine) 8, 130–31
Negro Digest 69–70
New York Magazine 79, 123
New York Times (newspaper) 7, 97, 112, 119
New Yorker (magazine) 2, 5, 7, 75, 81, 86, 94, 122
Newhouse Family 87, 94–5, 103–104, 106–107
News Corp. 87, 91–2, 100–101
newsstands 3, 5, 8, 22, 26, 30, 68, 111, 123

Pathfinder (online service) 97–100
People (magazine) 6–9, 13–16, 20–8, 30, 34–5, 79–81, 83, 86
Petersen, Anne Helen 32–3, 35, 40

Playboy (magazine) 5, 72–3, 111, 128
Pulitzer Prize 53, 115
Putnam's Monthly 57–9

Rogin, Gil 34, 38
Ryan, Pat 13–14, 29, 80

Selling Culture: Magazines, Markets and Class at the Turn of the Century (Ohmann) 64, 68
social media 7, 27, 40, 113, 128, 131
Spectator (magazine) 3, 44–5
Sports Illustrated 6, 21, 25, 34, 36, 40, 77
Steele, Richard 3, 44–7 *see also Tatler*
Stolley, Dick 13, 34–6, 38, 83, 85, 130

Tarbell, Ida 65–6 *see also* fiction in magazines
Tatler (magazine) 3, 44
Time Inc. 2, 6, 13, 16–20, 23–5, 28–30, 34, 36–40, 77, 80–2, 86–8, 97–100, 103
Time magazine 6, 8, 21, 25, 40, 50, 73–7, 80, 83, 85, 98, 115
Time Warner 28, 41, 96–100 *see also* Pathfinder
Time & Life Building 6, 30, 34, 38, 79
TV Guide 5–6, 13, 17–18, 27, 87–89, 91–2, 102
TV-Cable Week 17–18, 28, 88, 97

United States Magazine 43, 126
US Civil War 48, 51, 54–5
US Postal Act of 1794 51–2
US Postal Service 57, 61, 72 *see also* Bradford, Andrew; Comstock, Anthony

Vogue (magazine) 5, 7, 86, 94–5, 105, 107, 111, 124

Webster, Noah 3, 50–1, 54–5, 73
Westmark, Tamara 30

Yahoo 95, 100
Yong, Ed 118–19

Zuckerberg, Mark 76, 101–102